Ian Botham

Ian Botham

Bob Farmer

Hamlyn

London · New York · Sydney · Toronto

Published by
The Hamlyn Publishing Group Limited
London · New York · Sydney · Toronto
Astronaut House, Feltham, Middlesex, England

Filmset in England by
Photocomp Limited, Birmingham

Printed in England by
R. J. Acford, Chichester

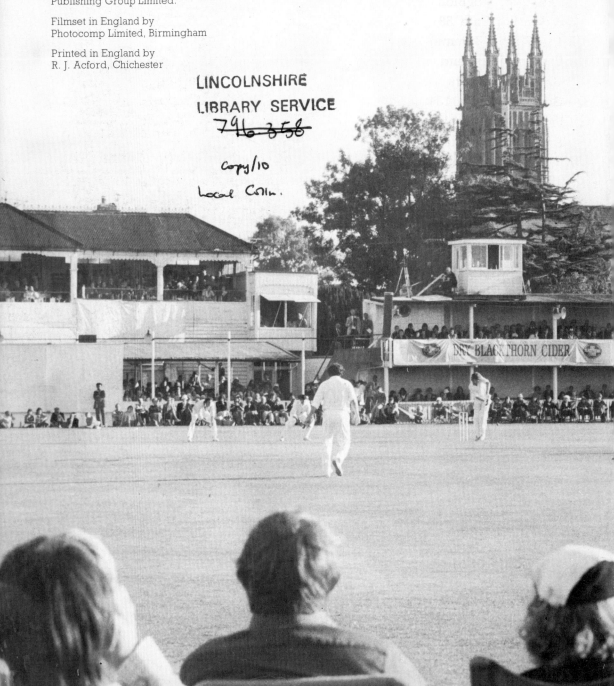

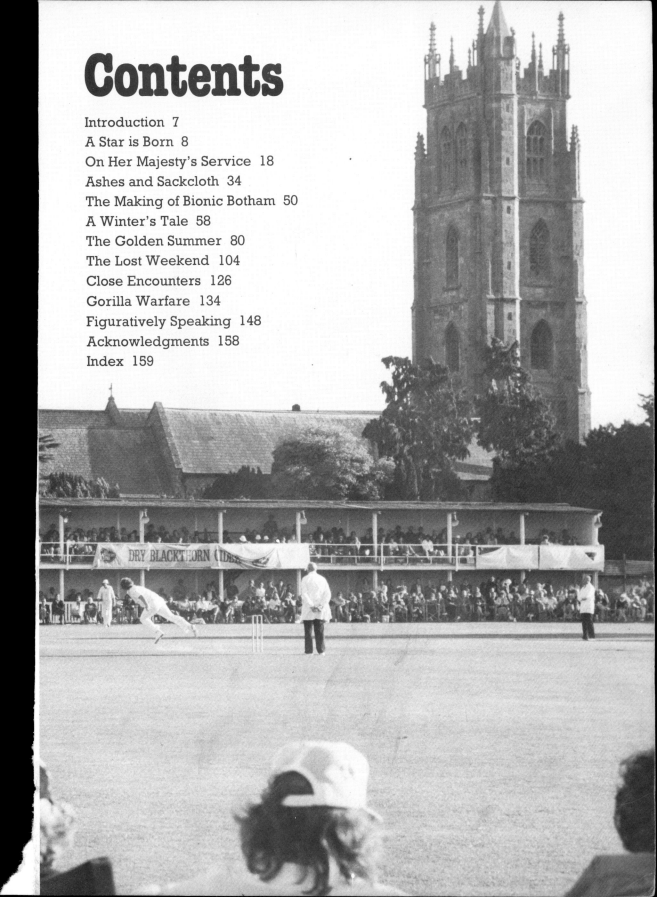

Contents

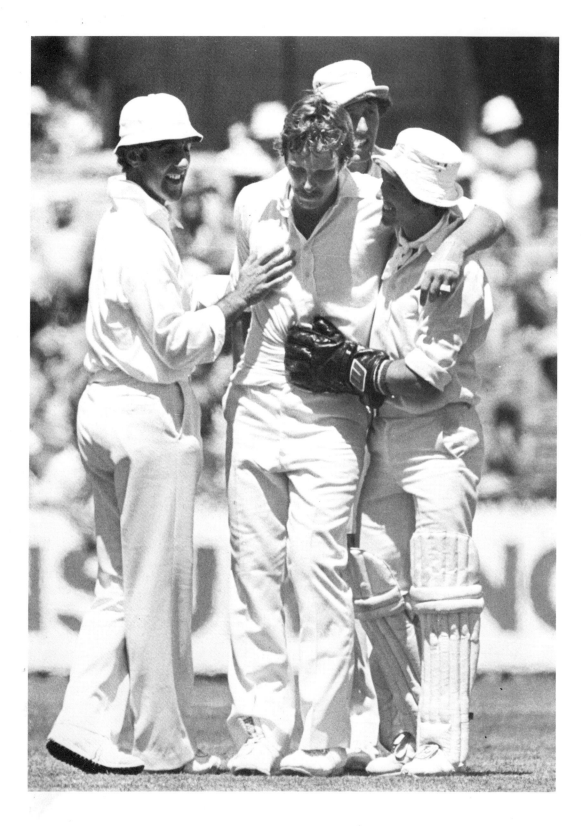

Introduction

There cannot have been many books written about the life and career of a person still in his early twenties. But Ian Terence Botham is quite a cricketer.

To the inevitable criticism that it is presumptuous and premature to praise the achievements of someone so young as Ian, I would only say that the British are far too self-deprecating when it comes to considering their own successes, and that the exploits of Ian really are something to shout about. No other cricketer has ever done so much in so short a time.

Who cares that sometimes his bowling goes astray and he gets clouted all over the field? Who cares that he will sometimes throw away his wicket with a wildly reckless shot? Whenever Ian is around something is bound to happen because he cannot bear to be out of the action.

What makes Ian's exploits the more enjoyable is the boyish innocence, burning enthusiasm and blatant joy he gets out of the game. He has captured the imagination of the youth of the country much more than any synthetic pop star ever could, because he has stepped straight from the pages of *Boys' Own*. He is larger than life and a winner.

There are, of course, the dismal johnnies who predict life will not always be a bowl of cherries for Ian Botham, that there must come occasions, as with all cricketers, when nothing will go right for him. Well, that has not happened yet, but – and possibly because they have a point – it is surely all the more reason to salute this splendid young sportsman while he is riding so high.

This book catalogues a meteoric career first with Somerset and then with England up to and including his part in the fight for the Ashes in the winter of 1978-79, and finally assesses the Ian Botham behind the startling statistics, in which I was much assisted by the knowledge of Brian Close, his county captain, who played such an important part in Ian's development.

Finally, to those of my colleagues who bore the brunt of my constant campaign for the Boy Wonder, I can only say: I told you so!

February 1979

A Star is Born

Wednesday, 12 June 1974 had been a brilliantly hot day, a glorious twelfth indeed, but now, as the shadows started piercing the quaint and rather ramshackle Taunton County Cricket Ground, all the fond hopes of a fitting finale to match such marvellous weather were dissolving into deep disappointment. Somerset, from a position of great strength, were in the process of throwing away their Benson and Hedges Cup quarter-final tie against Hampshire.

They had been handsomely placed at twenty minutes to twelve that morning when, in the space of ten minutes, Hampshire had lost the cream of their batting – Gordon Greenidge, Barry Richards, David Turner and Richard Gilliat – while the score remained static on 22. Then Trevor Jesty and Peter Sainsbury took root and repaired the innings to such effect that it was 31 overs and 95 runs before the next wicket fell. Jesty, revelling as ever against his favourite county opposition, went on to make 79 and, when Hampshire were eventually bowled out in the 54th over of this 55-over tie, their total of 182 represented a remarkable recovery.

By 5.30 in the evening it had become a positively match-winning position for, in the face of the ever-accurate Hampshire attack, Somerset, by a process of panic and poor batting, had utterly thrown away the initiative and slid to 113 for seven.

At this point entered a big, brash-looking 18-year-old, his bat windmilling vigorously as he exercised his broad shoulders. Ian Botham's arrival aroused no enthusiasm among Somerset's disconsolate supporters and it was not hard to understand why. Admittedly, the Yeovil youngster had bowled with great enthusiasm, sharing a part in Hampshire's earlier collapse and coming back to break the Jesty–Sainsbury stand. His final figures had been 11–3–33–2, and he had also shone with his athletic deep fielding although, in a team containing such senior citizens as Brian Close, Jim Parks, Tom Cartwright, Graham Burgess and Mervyn Kitchen, it would have been somewhat surprising if he had not been able to cut a dash in the deep.

Botham had played in only four first-class fixtures, scoring 13, 2, 26, 2 and 1. He had bowled 53 overs, taking just one wicket for 154 runs. The rest of his experience amounted to four John Player League appearances and a solitary game in the Benson and Hedges qualifying competition – ironically against Hampshire – when he had scarcely distinguished himself with a bowling return of one for 52 from 11 overs and an innings of 3.

Small wonder, then, that Somerset supporters were unexcited as he approached the middle. It was even a little puzzling that he was playing in so important a match. Presumably, with

Previous spread: A star is born. Ian Botham after his brave 45 not out had won a Benson and Hedges Cup quarter-final against Hampshire at Taunton in 1974.

so many elder statesmen in the side, his youth and vitality were considered necessary to give some edge to Somerset's fielding in a competition where fleetness of foot and the saving of runs often determine the result.

The batsmen had crossed during the fall of Somerset's seventh wicket and so Botham was not obliged immediately to face the bowling. Instead the greying Tom Cartwright, head hidden under a cap to shield him from the sun, swung with the sort of reckless abandon that admits defeat at Jesty's next delivery and skied to deep mid-on where Herman comfortably took the catch. The crestfallen Cartwright, who had already spent many hours attempting to improve Botham's bowling action, walked away without scoring and the score was 113 for eight.

Fifteen overs remained, 70 runs were required, but this was academic information. How on earth could an inexperienced youngster like Botham be expected to enact a miracle with only Hallam Moseley and Bob Clapp – two of the rankest tailenders in county cricket – to support him?

A few supporters started to give their answer by shuffling out of the ground and round to the Ring of Bells up the road. A quick pint before the crowds packed in seemed preferable to waiting for the inevitable end. What they were to miss over the next hour will forever remain a bitter regret in their cricketing memories.

With the West Indian Moseley stubbornly sticking a bat at all balls on line and leaving well alone when he did not have to play a shot, Botham immediately began laying about him. Probably it was born of a feeling that there was nothing really left to lose and his side might as well die defiant. It was when he heaved his first massive six high over square leg and out of the ground that Botham began to believe in himself. Much more important, he began to sense an outrageous victory.

With Moseley now taking up the mood as well and pushing ones and twos, the score started creeping up and after 45 overs had advanced to 131 for eight.

Now, however, disaster arrived as the much-feared Andy Roberts was brought into the attack to end this impudent resistance. Roberts had arrived in the English game that summer, an unknown Antiguan who had quickly established himself as the most hostile fast bowler any English batsman had encountered since the Australian Dennis Lillee. Even the much-admired Colin Cowdrey had recently been felled at Basingstoke ('I took the ball on the chin, spreadeagled my stumps, cracked a few teeth and took an involuntary count of about a hundred and ten,' he wryly recalls).

Above: The great Barry Richards cannot believe it . . . bowled by a raw unknown and the Hampshire slide is on. David Turner is the other batsman.

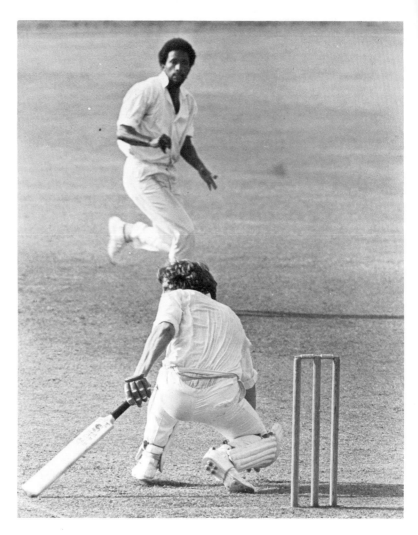

Moment of impact. Ian drops on one knee as a ball from Andy Roberts smacks him in the face.

Roberts dug in a vicious short-lifter, the young Botham bravely went to hook where others would have put personal safety first and ducked, and the crack on the side of his face could be heard all round a hushed Taunton ground. Blood started seeping from gums and lips; he half staggered. Gilliat hastily gathered his fielders around Botham like some funeral cortège preparing to lift the coffin, but the boy foolhardily waved away suggestions that he should go off with the angry assertion that he was all right. In fact, he was to lose four teeth.

'I didn't know a lot about it,' he recalls. 'I was definitely a bit concussed, but,' so brashly, 'hits on the head are usually quite safe.'

He also adds today: 'With more experience, probably I should have retired.' That is totally untrue and mere modesty. Today he would have done what he did then – stay at the crease.

So Botham stayed and, perhaps in painful anger, really started to propel the score. Overs 45 to 50 produced 34 runs including another enormous Botham six and suddenly Somerset were into the last five overs needing only 18 more runs to win.

The ground was agog, Hampshire fielders were running about in near-hysteria at the totally unexpected turn of events, but Roberts had returned for the final three overs of his allocation of eleven and, at last, he had some reward.

The gallant Moseley was nailed leg before with a ball which kept low at the start of the 53rd over. The Barbadian had hit 24 crucial runs – one of his highest scores in limited-overs cricket – in a thirteen-over stand of 63. The applause from the 6,500 crowd was warm, but now it was Somerset's turn to be desperate again as the initiative swung back to Hampshire.

For the incoming batsman was Bob Clapp, a gangling fast-

medium bowler whose career-best contribution with the bat was 1 not out. Now he had to face the fury of the fastest bowler in county cricket. Gilliat almost gloatingly called up his field for the *coup de grâce*. Roberts roared in, Clapp despairingly tried to dig the ball out, but it struck him on the pad and squirted towards square leg and the now galvanic Botham almost screamed for the leg bye that would give him the bowling.

177 for nine – six runs wanted and Botham defended until the last ball of the over. It was up to him to keep Clapp away from the strike and as Roberts bounded in again Botham got a good sighting and smote hard into the outfield. There were easily two runs in the shot, but Botham needed the third run to keep the strike. Clapp was the one who had to beat the throw and he used his long legs to great effect as he flung himself headlong for the crease in a cloud of dust as wicketkeeper Bob Stephenson whipped off the bails with a frenzied appeal. Not out!

Above: The winning hit off Herman. Ian sets out for glory, and Bob Clapp has almost reached the other end.

So it was now 180 for nine with two overs to go. The Hampshire trustie Bob Herman bowled to Botham, but induced no shot as he pitched outside off stump. It was the same with the next ball, but the third and fourth and fifth had Somerset and Hampshire hearts in their mouths. Botham heaved frantically at each and failed to connect. Each could have been a catch behind; each could have been a decisive boundary. One ball left and then it would be Roberts, all fire and brimstone, to bowl the last over to the defenceless Clapp. It was now or never.

'Keep your head' . . . 'have a go' . . . the boy's brain was in a whirl under fevered exhortations of the fans. Whether Herman had fractionally overpitched or not, Botham went again for the big one – and connected bang in the meat and middle of the bat. The ball was scorching over the outfield before cover could move and leapt like a salmon as it smacked into the boundary rope to a mighty roar from the crowd.

15

The next few seconds were pure pandemonium. Botham, arms aloft, ran helter skelter through the engulfing fans to the preserves of the pavilion, where he was promptly propelled back out in front of the fans by his delighted team-mates. The Gold Award adjudicator, Charlie Barnett, the old Gloucestershire player, made himself heard above the din. Pausing only to praise both teams for what he termed one of the most exciting matches ever seen at Taunton, Barnett turned to Botham and said: 'Today we saw a young man who batted with great bravery for his 45 not out and also bowled and fielded with great spirit. I think we are going to hear a lot more of Ian Botham!'

By nightfall a new star was twinkling brightly in cricket's firmament. Much more would be heard of Botham.

Well done, kid! A slap on the back from Clapp as the Botham fan-club show their faces for the first time.

Hampshire Taunton June 12

Hampshire

Richards, B		b Botham	13
Greenidge	c Cartwright	b Burgess	9
Turner		run out	0
Gilliat	c Moseley	b Burgess	0
Jesty	c Burgess	b Moseley	79
Sainsbury	c Richards	b Botham	40
Lewis	c Taylor	b Clapp	25
Taylor, M	c Taylor	b Moseley	0
Stephenson		run out	0
Roberts	c Taylor	b Moseley	4
Herman		not out	6
Extras (lb 1, w 5)			6
Total (53·3 overs)			182

Fall of wickets: 1–22, 2–22, 3–22, 4–22, 5–117, 6–157, 7–158, 8–171, 9–173

Bowling: Clapp 10–0–43–1, Moseley 10·3–2–28–3, Botham 11–3–33–2, Burgess 11–1–52–2, Cartwright 11–4–20–0

Somerset

Umpires
G. H. Pope
R. Julian

Gold Award
Ian Botham

Kitchen	c Gilliat	b Herman	5
Taylor, D	c Richards	b Taylor	33
Denning		b Jesty	11
Richards, V	c Stephenson	b Jesty	1
Close		b Roberts	28
Parks	c Herman	b Jesty	9
Burgess	lbw	b Sainsbury	13
Cartwright	c Herman	b Jesty	0
Botham		not out	45
Moseley	lbw	b Roberts	24
Clapp		not out	0
Extras (b 1, lb 12, nb 2)			15
Total (9 wickets – 54 overs)			184

Fall of wickets: 1–9, 2–33, 3–37, 4–85, 5–89, 6–113, 7–113, 8–113, 9–176

Bowling: Roberts 10–2–26–2, Herman 11–1–40–1, Taylor 11–1–50–1, Jesty 11–2–28–4, Sainsbury 11–2–25–1

Somerset won by one wicket

On Her Majesty's Service

As Ian Botham boarded the flight to Adelaide, Australia, in October 1978 for the fight for the Ashes, albeit with his left arm in a sling after an unfortunate farewell night out with the boys two days earlier in Doncaster, it was not inappropriate to compare him with a colossus about to bestride the world. At the still absurdly young age of 22 he had become larger than life, the unquestioned idol of British schoolboys, a man able easily to finish far in front of footballers in the various popularity polls, the biggest crowd draw in cricket, a Croesus among the collectors of awards in a game now happily and healthily weighed down with precious perks dangled by an unending assembly line of cricket-conscious sponsors.

This startingly rapid superstar status had been achieved in a mere twelve months. Yet Ian was able to reflect during the flight to Adelaide that he had been compelled to play a patient waiting game before another hesitant England selection panel had decided to plunge him into Test cricket in 1977.

English selection attitudes are anathema to Australians. They are baffling to all but officialdom in England, too. The Antipodean attitude is that if a youngster shows exceptional promise, then put him into the Test team and hope for a dividend. He will sink or swim by his own ability and he will enjoy an extended period to prove himself. This enterprising attitude brought about the selection of raw talent like Ron Hammence (the batsman who always baffles the compilers of Bradman's famous 1948 touring party in their pub conversation pieces), more familiar names like Ian Craig and Norman O'Neill and, in contemporary cricket, David Hookes.

England's selectors, admittedly, showed the same bold approach when the fledgling Brian Close was flung into the Australian cauldron on the 1950-51 tour, following his Test baptism the previous summer at the age of 18, still the youngest player to be picked by England. The experiment was a failure, but senior players in the party, by their failure to encourage the youngster, took their share of the blame. Close still claims

bitterly today: 'Natural ability is only a part of the whole that makes a good cricketer. This is a difficult game to learn – a game that is so involved that it takes a long, long time to start to get to know what it's all about. As an inexperienced youngster I was looking for guidance on that first overseas tour – I didn't get it.'

Whatever the criticism of his playing qualities and qualifications for Test cricket, England's Mike Brearley can justifiably claim to captain a very happy band in which everyone helps out each other. Ian Botham is fortunate to have been given his big chance under Brearley's leadership.

After the unsuccessful Close experiment of 1950-51, however, the England selectors went through many years of quite bizarre decisions which began, at a time of poor playing results, with the resuscitation of 42-year-old Cyril Washbrook five years after he had left the international scene and culminated in the call-up of the self-same Close when he was 45 to bear the brunt of the West Indian fast bowling ferocity that was overwhelming England in 1976.

So when Botham was brought to Test recognition in 1977 it was to be hoped that short-sighted selectorial attitudes like this had ended. Indeed, the arrival of the even younger David Gower of Leicestershire in 1978 suggested the selectors had at last latched on to the need to throw youngsters into Test cricket

Previous spread: Meeting The Queen on his Test debut at Trent Bridge in July 1977.

This spread: By mid '78 Ian had all the trappings of success: a TR7 to announce his affluence (*below*), headline proof of his rich pickings (*top right*), and gifts from his sponsors, Rank Radio International (*bottom right*).

and hope for the best. Botham and Gower both produced results at once to become the stars of the summer.

England were producing a series of splendid young players. However, as the 1978 plane flew on to Adelaide, with both Botham and Gower aboard because of their unquestionable ability, the bad old ways seemed to be back. Where on the plane were such outstanding youngsters as Yorkshire's 19-year-old Kevin Sharp, Kent's Chris Tavare, 24, Northants' Wayne Larkins, 25, Middlesex's Mike Gatting, 21, possibly even Ian's Somerset team-mate Peter Roebuck, 22? What had happened to Kent wicketkeeper Paul Downton, dropped at 21 after being sent on the previous winter's Pakistan/New Zealand tour then cursorily overlooked again? England's second string wicket-keeper to the 37-year-old Bob Taylor was, with due deference to his abilities, the 32-year-old Roger Tolchard. The England selectors do not have to justify themselves in public over their appointments, otherwise it would have been illuminating to hear their explanations for the appointment of two wicket-keepers in the first flushes of middle age.

Ian's own claims had become incontestable by 1977 and fortunately he hit the jackpot right away. Without such immediate success it is an interesting thought that this book could not have been written today. Such a thought seems, to me, to underline the absurdity of England selection attitudes, as the unfortunate Paul Downton, if he wanted to rock the boat and ruin his career, would be able to testify.

The success Botham enjoyed and the strides he had made, however, since the announcement of his ability three years earlier in that Hampshire match, made his case in 1977 incontestable.

So it was that, under the banner headline GIVE IAN A CHANCE in the *Daily Mirror* of Friday, 15 July 1977, with the sub heading 'Hero Botham ready for an England cap', I had been able to write: 'The England selectors can surely ignore Ian Botham no longer.'

He had just hit an unbeaten 91 to win a Gillette Cup tie for his county against Northumberland at Taunton. Not the most exacting of opposition, one may say, but Somerset had made unexpectedly heavy weather of winning. They were 26 for three, chasing a modest target of 154 with the redoubtable Viv Richards among the early victims.

I wrote: 'It called for a cool head and immense character to stop a sensation. Botham has both. The big Yeovil youngster thumped 14 fours, finished the match with a straight six into the pavilion and emphasised to all that, with Tony Greig disgraced over the Packer affair and in the doghouse over his opinion of the

Old Trafford pitch (an allusion to undiplomatic remarks Greig had made about the state of the second Test wicket), Botham must be ready to replace him.'

The Northumberland innings, of course, was not the criterion upon which to judge Ian's claim for a place in the England team. Right from the start of 1977, after an invaluable winter in Australia being taught his bowling trade by the legendary Frank Tyson – thanks to the admirable Whitbread Trust scheme to give promising young English county cricketers 'scholarships' down under – Botham had positively bubbled.

He had played for MCC in the traditional season's opening challenge match against the county champions Middlesex and

Cutting everyone else down to size. A cracking four for MCC in the 1977 season curtain-raiser against Middlesex.

The power and the glory. A tremendous four off Kerry O'Keeffe, all part of Somerset's historic victory over the Australians at Bath in 1977. Marsh is the wicketkeeper.

stolen the show with a belligerent unbeaten 53 in 75 minutes, which he supplemented with five wickets in a rain-ruined match.

Then, in a memorable match at Bath, Botham had played a princely part as Somerset, by some seven wickets, beat an Australian touring team for the first time in their long history. He had taken Jeff 'Terror' Thomson apart, torn into the spinners and made a magnificent run-a-minute 59 which included three sixes and six fours. Then he attacked again to finish things off on the final day with 39 of the last 53 runs needed for victory.

MCC were to spot another side to his skills as he took five catches, some in the slips, some in the deep, in another traditional match, the Test warm-up with the Australians at Lord's.

So it was no surprise, after that Northumberland headline, that, two days later, the England selectors agreed it was, indeed, time to 'give Ian a chance'.

I had travelled to Hove that Sunday morning, where Somerset were playing a John Player League match, to get an immediate reaction from the young man of the moment. It was hardly the occasion for the crowning of a new cricket king. It was more a question of the Emperor's new clothes. Ian was in his underpants, the rain was slanting down outside, and Geoff Boycott was really the big story since he had been led back into the Test side like the prodigal son after four years of self-imposed exile. So, apart from expressing his obvious delight, Ian was cautious enough to admit: 'I'll probably finish up being twelfth man.'

His tempered enthusiasm was not without explanation. Earlier in the summer he had been selected for England's squad in the three one-day internationals, but his only intrusion on the playing area had been to bear out the drinks tray. Another opportunity to test a bright youngster, if only in one of the limited-over matches had again been inexplicably ignored. Now he was only in the third Test squad because of a doubt about the fitness of the Yorkshire all-rounder Chris Old. Tony Greig, true, had lost face, but not his place.

Old, however, was unfit and on a sunny 28 July morning Ian learned his big moment had finally arrived. Then a strange, quite uncharacteristic event occurred. He lost his nerve. The big and brash, forceful and fearless Botham was suffering stage fright.

He says today: 'I suppose I've turned out to be a bit of a big match player. I had that bad time in the pavilion at Nottingham because I didn't quite know how I would react.'

It was his regular England room-mate Mike Hendrick, the Derbyshire fast bowler, who calmed him down. 'He asked me how the shooting (a favourite pastime of Ian's) was going. He has a shotgun and does a bit himself. We talked about shooting and I got very calm.'

So, shortly before 11.30 am Ian trooped out with the rest of the England team into the arena of a Trent Bridge ground of which the gates were to be closed before lunch for the first time since Bradman's all-conquering Aussies had been there in 1948. Willis and Hendrick could make no early impression and the Australian opening pair, McCosker and Davis, had given their side their best start in the series when skipper Brearley brought on the fledgling Botham as first-change bowler. McCosker edged Botham's second ball to where third slip would have been, but this initial encouragement was of no avail. The youngster started spraying far too many deliveries down the legside or pitching short and he suffered some severe punishment. Botham's first spell in Test cricket was becoming a slight

The schoolboys' idol. A convoy of porters escort Botham on arrival at Taunton.

embarrassment by the time Brearley took him off and went instead for the slow left-arm Underwood.

If Ian was entitled to feel somewhat deflated, his guardian angel, as ever, was hovering overhead. Twenty minutes before lunch, with the opening stand now an ominous 79, Underwood drew Davis forward too soon with his slower delivery and the ball lobbed up into a mercifully easy catch to Botham at mid-on. At least he had now made a contribution although, at 101 for one, he hardly went to lunch in a particularly happy frame of mind.

So it stayed until 3.15 pm and the pause for drinks. McCosker, by now, had gone, but at 131 for two, Australia could anticipate a powerful position by the close of play. Botham had not been brought back to bowl, but, the drinks downed, Brearley tossed the ball to him again. His first delivery was so short that the 22,000 crowd groaned and waited for Greg Chappell, the Australian captain, to grind it into the cover boundary. Greg, however, leaned back too lazily and chopped

Fleet Street greets the young hero. Although the broadcasters say 'Boatham', the *Express* have it right in this favourite Test debut tribute.

the ball into his stumps. The guardian angel was working
overtime.

There followed, in the time-honoured cliché of all chroniclers
of sporting sagas, the sort of heroics that belong only in the
pages of *Boys' Own*. In 34 balls Botham was to produce the
startling spell of four wickets for 13 runs. As Ian started to swing
the ball away from the off-stump, Doug Walters followed it
wildly and Hendrick took a straightforward slip catch. Then the
aggressive, untidy Rodney Marsh prodded, missed and was
plumb leg before, finally Max Walker hung out his bat and
Hendrick (what a boost he was proving to Botham this day)
again accepted the slip catch. With Hookes and Robinson
accounted for at the other end, Australia had slid sensationally
to 155 for eight.

The stand that followed was inevitably broken when Botham
had Jeff Thomson taken behind – Australia 196 for nine – before
play was brought to a halt ('Reign Stops Play' said the agency
flash to newspapers) by the arrival of The Queen, interrupting
an East Midlands tour to mark her Silver Jubilee celebrations,
to be introduced to the two teams.

In the background for once (*extreme right*) as Geoff Boycott goes centre stage to greet the cheers for the Trent Bridge Test win.

As ever she had been well briefed. Pausing before the new boy wonder of English cricket, she said to Ian: 'It looks as if you've been doing some work.' Indeed he had. Australia were all out that evening for 243, Botham had figures of 20–5–74–5 and the next morning the newspapers were ecstatic. 'Howzatta Boy' hailed the *Daily Express* in a centre spread splash as they explained: 'England find the man to take over from Tony Greig'.

Howzat, indeed, for a right royal day!

The *Express*, however, had been premature in supposing him automatically to be the heir apparent to the 'big, bad Greig'. He had yet to show his credentials as an all-rounder by succeeding with the bat, and because of what befell England on the second day he did not have much time to bask in the glory of his great deeds the day before. From an overnight nine for no wicket, England, by early afternoon, had slid to a dismal 82 for five under the relentless attack of Thomson, Pascoe and the persevering Walker. Botham, due in next, would be the last of the England line-up with any batting ability, and it appeared that all the pressure that had disappeared with his five for 74 was about to pile up on him again as the last hope of helping his side to a respectable score. And a few minutes later his heart skipped a beat as Boycott palpably edged Pascoe to McCosker at second slip. The catch went down. Boycott, too, has his own guardian angel.

The Yorkshireman dug even more determinedly into his crease. He had that admirable little fighter, Alan Knott, as his sixth-wicket partner and together they survived until tea. Australian heads, never high in 1977, now began to drop as Boycott and Knott became ever more confident so that, when bad light brought the close forward by half an hour, England were only one run behind, Boycott on 88, Knott 87, Botham still sitting there in the players' balcony with his pads on.

While Botham had enjoyed unreserved acclaim for his deeds, however, Boycott had been labouring since long before lunch under the unhappy burden of being responsible for the running out of the local idol, Derek Randall. He had been warmly welcomed back to the Test arena, but a century now was essential after such an indiscretion and, to the manner born, Boycott duly accomplished his ninety-ninth first-class hundred the following morning, only to get himself out shortly afterwards at 297.

So, at last, the alleged all-rounder was on his way out to the wicket with 50 minutes to survive until lunch and England still in need of some more runs to make their first innings lead a worthwhile one. He was demonstrably nervous and now again that guardian angel stepped in to save him. Thomson, tail up for the raw newcomer, was bowling and his third ball unerringly found the edge of Botham's bat and flew easily enough to that soundest of slip fielders, Chappell. It went into his hands and out again.

When Ian was still a schoolboy – 'Dad,' he'd said one day, 'I may not have very good marks, but it doesn't matter because I'm going to make cricket my career' – he had been able to watch this same Greg Chappell taking his own first exploratory steps in cricket as a Somerset player. Chappell had enjoyed his time there, but such benevolence to a fellow Wessex Wyvern was really rather overdoing it. Not only had his careless stroke given Ian his first Test wicket off a rank bad ball two days earlier and thus inspired the youngster, but he had now reprieved Botham off a rank bad shot.

It was an escape gratefully accepted. After lunch and after 'Knotty' had departed for 135, the highest innings by an England wicketkeeper against Australia, Botham became the boss with only Underwood, Hendrick and Willis left to bat. He hit out boldly, three scorching fours through the covers again earning that comparison with Greig before the weary Walker bowled him for a completely satisfactory 25.

England, at 364, had earned a first innings lead of 121 and although the Australians, principally inspired by McCosker's 107, made a stout fight of their second innings, with Botham unable to achieve a breakthrough although bowled for 25 overs, the victory target of 189 was made simple by a Brearley–Boycott stand of 154. England got home on the final afternoon by some seven wickets, they were two-nil up in the series and Ian Botham knew he had done more than enough to ensure he would be part of the team attempting to win back the Ashes in 12 days' time.

The Third Test Trent Bridge

Australia
1st innings

Close of play
First Day
England 9–0
Brearley 5 not out
Boycott 4 not out

McCosker	c Brearley	b Hendrick	51
Davis	c Botham	b Underwood	33
Chappell		b Botham	19
Hookes	c Hendrick	b Willis	17
Walters	c Hendrick	b Botham	11
Robinson	c Brearley	b Greig	11
Marsh	lbw	b Botham	0
O'Keeffe		not out	48
Walker	c Hendrick	b Botham	0
Thomson	c Knott	b Botham	21
Pascoe	c Greig	b Hendrick	20
Extras (b 4, lb 2, nb 6)			12
Total			**243**

Fall of wickets: 1–79, 2–101, 3–131, 4–133, 5–153, 6–153, 7–153, 8–155, 9–196
Bowling: Willis 15–0–58–1, Hendrick 21·2–6–46–2, Botham 20–5–74–5, Greig 15–4–35–1, Underwood 11–5–18–1

2nd innings

Close of play
Third Day
Australia 112–2
McCosker 40 not out
Hookes 31 not out

Umpires
H. D. Bird
D. J. Constant

McCosker	c Brearley	b Willis	107
Davis	c Greig	b Willis	9
Chappell		b Hendrick	27
Hookes	lbw	b Hendrick	42
Walters	c Randall	b Greig	28
Robinson	lbw	b Underwood	34
Marsh	c Greig	b Willis	0
O'Keeffe		not out	21
Walker		b Willis	17
Thomson		b Willis	0
Pascoe	c Hendrick	b Underwood	0
Extras (b 1, lb 5, w 1, nb 17)			24
Total			**309**

Fall of wickets: 1–18, 2–60, 3–154, 4–204, 5–240, 6–240, 7–270, 8–307, 9–308
Bowling: Willis 26–6–88–5, Hendrick 32–14–56–2, Botham 25–5–60–0, Greig 9–2–24–1, Underwood 27–15–49–2, Miller 5–2–5–0, Woolmer 3–0–3–0

July 28, 29, 30 August 1, 2

England
1st innings

Second Day
England 242–5
Boycott 88 not out
Knott 87 not out

Brearley	c Hookes	b Pascoe	15
Boycott	c McCosker	b Thomson	107
Woolmer	lbw	b Pascoe	0
Randall		run out	13
Greig		b Thomson	11
Miller	c Robinson	b Pascoe	13
Knott	c Davis	b Thomson	135
Botham		b Walker	25
Underwood		b Pascoe	7
Hendrick		b Walker	1
Willis		not out	2
Extras (b 8, lb 7, w 3, nb 16)			35
Total			**364**

Fall of wickets: 1–34, 2–34, 3–52, 4–64, 5–82, 6–297, 7–326, 8–357, 9–357
Bowling: Thomson 31–6–103–3, Pascoe 32–10–80–4, Walker 39·2–12–79–2, Chappell 8–0–19–0, O'Keeffe 11–4–43–0, Walters 3–0–5–0

2nd innings

Target 189

Close of play
Fourth Day
England 17–0
Brearley 5 not out
Boycott 12 not out

Brearley		b Walker	81
Boycott		not out	80
Knott	c O'Keeffe	b Walker	2
Greig		b Walker	0
Randall		not out	19
Woolmer			
Miller			
Botham			
Underwood			
Hendrick			
Willis			
Extras (b 2, lb 2, w 1, nb 2)			7
Total		(3 wickets)	**189**

Fall of wickets: 1–154, 2–160, 3–165
Bowling: Thomson 16–6–34–0, Pascoe 22–6–43–0, Walker 24–8–40–3, O'Keeffe 19·2–2–65–0

England won by 7 wickets

Ashes and Sackcloth

Confidence is all in cricket and Ian Botham has it in bucketfuls. One could see it in the way he walked out to bat next day amid the applause of an alien crowd for his achievements over the previous weekend at Trent Bridge.

He had not, in fact, had far to travel from the scene of his triumph, a mere few miles out of Nottingham to the unlovely Derbyshire town of Ilkeston to do battle on behalf of Somerset again in an important Gillette Cup quarter-final tie. It was a difficult draw, but a rather fitting reward for the fumbling win over Northumberland in the previous round.

A long journey, however, would hardly have worried Ian. Contemporary cricketers are all too aware of the taxing travelling their trade entails. Certainly, stepping from a five-day Test straight into the diverse demands of an important one-day Cup-tie is a strenuous exercise, but the first-class game these days is played under extreme pressures.

The old jibe that cricket is a leisurely occupation by comparison with such sports, say, as soccer, rugby or athletics just is not applicable any more. The accompanying cracks that cricketers can carry on into their late thirties or early forties because of the sedate nature of the sport are equally spurious.

Once the first-class season is under way, county cricketers are almost constantly playing from day to day for a full four months. Because of the great importance attached to the limited-overs game with its accent on fast scoring and fleet running between the wickets and in the field, the unfit player will soon find his place in the team under pressure.

It does not help these demands on the player, either, that because of the heavy fixture programme an inordinate amount of travelling is involved whereby, in a weekend, he can finish a home county match on a Friday, travel off the same night for the start of an away three-day match the following day, come off the field at the close on Saturday and straight into the car to drive to a Sunday League fixture and be back to continue the three-day game on the Monday. On top of all that travelling, he also has his

form to worry about. It all suggests to me that ageless legends like Brian Close, Basil d'Oliveira and others will not be a part of the game in future years because the body can stand only so much. Even Ian Botham was to experience the strain in 1977.

However, Ian went to Ilkeston under no such strain and his county colleagues, too, had arrived hale if not hearty. Their previous Championship match had been scheduled to end, like the Test, on Tuesday, but they had been not long detained in Lancashire, having lost in under two days, their second innings expiring in precisely 84 minutes. Some fierce fast bowling by Colin Croft and Peter Lee split the little finger of Viv Richards and caused captain Brian Close to mutter blackly about the state of Southport wickets.

They had slipped from fourth to seventh in the table and could entertain no longer any lingering hopes of keeping up with the leaders. So, all things considered, the ship was hardly seaworthy for a day-long voyage against a Derbyshire side up and coming under the leadership of the South African all-rounder Eddie Barlow.

Instead, Somerset thrived after Close had won the toss and elected to bat. By the time Botham was called on to come in at No 4, the total was 163 for two in the 48th over.

Mainstay of the innings was the county's future captain, Brian Rose, who was out off the last ball of the innings for an admirable 128. Botham had been run out on the previous ball, but not before he had hoisted the only six of the match and had helped Rose add a riotous 85 in 12 overs. Against this imposing 248 for four, poor Derbyshire despaired, especially after Botham had nailed a glowering, disbelieving Barlow leg before to make it 11 for two.

Somerset eventually won by 59 runs, Rose collected the Man of the Match award, Close chuckled about never before having played a Gillette Cup tie in which he had not been called on to bat and Botham's stock just rose higher and higher.

After a weekend in the West Country – where opponents Northamptonshire beat Somerset out of sight in both Championship and Sunday League fixtures – Botham travelled north to join the England team for the fourth momentous Test at Headingley.

The expectancy in Leeds was electric, not just for the return of the Ashes, but also in the very real belief that Boycott's ton of tons would come before his own crowd. There was a challenge, too, for Botham. The hardened Headingley folk were only a portion of a sceptical public not yet prepared to swallow the praise that had been poured on him by the Press. He had not, either, achieved anything in county matches against Yorkshire

apart from an innings of 52 and that had been hit in the far west, away from the 'bright lights' of cricket.

In the event it was appropriately Boycott who was called on first to meet the hopes of Headingley and he could hardly have imagined a more unnerving beginning than the sight of his skipper, Brearley, who had taken strike, edging Thomson to Marsh off the third ball of the innings. Nowt for one, to localise the situation. This, though, only deepened Boycott's determination to do right by his own supporters.

Woolmer, in a second-wicket stand of 82, Randall in a regrettably short-lived stay of 23 runs, then the towering Greig (yes, he was still around in spite of himself) in a fourth-wicket partnership of 96, gave solid support. All the time Boycott quietly, methodically accumulated. Thirty-four runs before lunch, 69 by tea.

It was ten minutes to six when an enormous roar echoed around Leeds to emphasise the fact that Surrey's Graham Roope had written his name into the record books. That, at least, was the bizarre way of looking at it. On 12 July, the Surrey batsman had been at the other end as John Edrich, in front of the usual minimal smattering of Oval members, reached his hundredth hundred in a meaningless county match. Now, on 11 August, Roope was again at the other end as Boycott unerringly on-drove Chappell to the boundary to reach his own milestone. The applause lasted for six minutes, someone stole Geoffrey's cap and then rather shamefacedly brought it back. The TV cameras swung to the players' balcony and zoomed in on the applause. In the forefront was Botham and the shot is always shown in the re-runs of that epic occasion. Unwitting as Ian was, the shot has an amusing side to it, for in his first few Tests, at least, Botham and Boycott might appear to have upstaged each other in a manner that would do credit to a Crawford–Davis movie. A couple of more contradictory cricketers it would be hard to imagine, but unquestionably theirs are the names most readily identified with the game when one talks to youngsters. Boycott, perhaps, because of his imperious self-assurance about being the best English batsman in the business; Botham, because he comes straight out of the pages of boys' adventure books.

With Boycott 110 not out overnight, England 252 for four and many more runs to follow, it did seem that the unrecognised rivalry between the two would not show up in this Test. Boycott carried on relentlessly on the Friday and was within a whisker of reaching a double century and carrying his bat when he was quite unexpectedly last out for 191 caught by the suffering Chappell who was currently fielding at slip.

On your way, Aussie! David Hookes is lbw as umpire Alley confirms.

England had totalled 436 of which the Somerset youngster's contribution had been as abstract as that of his skipper Brearley . . . bowled by the bearded spinner Ray Bright without troubling the scorers.

An all-rounder's lot is a happy one, for failure with the bat always presents the early opportunity of redemption with the ball and Botham was to seize that chance with both hands, but even he could not have imagined what was to happen in the last 85 minutes of a traumatic day which would be long remembered in the cricketing annals of Australia.

Under the heavy cloud that has now become a hallmark of a heady bowling spell by Botham, it was his mate Hendrick who

The renowned rabbit. Doug Walters, as ever, edges (*above*), and Mike Hendrick, crouching at third slip (*right*), picks up another catch for Ian.

started the rout. His second ball had Davis leg before for a duck; his thirteenth had Chappell edging into the safe hands of Brearley at slip . . . 26 for 2. Willis, however, was getting stick from the determined McCosker, who had managed to distinguish himself in Australia's defeat at Trent Bridge with innings of 51 and 107, and inevitably first-change Botham was brought on for the 11th over.

The next England acclaim was, instead, for Randall as he ran out McCosker who had backed up too eagerly. But Botham, a duck behind him the same day, could not be kept out of action for long. By the close he had the young Australian hope Hookes hopelessly leg before and his dramatic swinging delivery again, as at Trent Bridge, had Walters unerringly edging into the hands of his trusty companion Hendrick.

Australia closed at 67 for five and the Hendrick–Botham attack was resumed next day with immediate results. Marsh, splendidly scruffy as ever, was first to fall, Knott the catcher, Botham the bowler. The same combination accounted for Walker while Botham needed no assistance in scattering Thomson's stumps.

Australia were all out for 103, Hendrick taking four for 41 and Botham the extraordinary analysis of 11–3–21–5. Up in the commentary box, Ian Chappell, who had only a short time

indus Findus

previously himself led one of the strongest Australian teams since 1948, now had the embarrassing task of talking to the television cameras about the total eclipse of the side being led by his brother Greg.

Ian Chappell had been a pugnacious captain who always played hard – perhaps too hard – to win, but he could point to outstanding Australian success since he had taken over the leadership after Ray Illingworth's England had snatched back the Ashes in 1970-71.

He eventually handed over to his younger brother, but was most obviously still the motivating force as Australia trounced West Indies 5–1 with unbelievable ease in 1975-76. Yet in the same season, as he was leading South Australia to convincing Sheffield Shield success, he picked a quarrel with his state's authorities over the omission of one of the side for their east coast fixtures, and at the end of the season he said he intended in future to restrict his cricket to club level. It was, of course, a smokescreen, soon to clear, for the emergence of the demon king, Kerry Packer.

So it was that, released of all responsibility to Australia, Chappell had come to England for the Ashes series and seemed an obvious candidate for television comments on the Tests.

Now, here at Headingley with Australia's reputation in ruins,

How are the mighty fallen! Out goes Marsh (*top left*), caught by Knott; Walker (*bottom left*) suffers the same fate, and (*above*) Thomson is ruthlessly removed as Ian reels off five for 21.

43

Master and pupil. Frank Tyson (*above*) bowling for England at Adelaide in 1954; (*above right*) Ian, twenty-four years later at Lord's, displays a similar action.

their team torn apart by the Packer revelations and the Ashes irretrievably in English hands again, Ian Chappell must almost have choked on his words as he was pressed by interviewer Peter West to talk about England's young 'discovery' Ian Botham.

It is one of cricket's not well-kept secrets that the Commonwealth ties between Britain and Australia were sorely strained one evening the preceding winter in Melbourne where Botham was spending his previously-mentioned Whitbread-sponsored scholarship under the tutelage of Frank Tyson.

The two Ians met and the subject of English cricket came up for conversation, Chappell being in the position to point out that England had only recently been quite overwhelmed by West Indies 3–0 just a few months after Australia had themselves drubbed West Indies 5–1.

The uncommitted would have to accept that Chappell had strong arguments to support his assessment of the Poms. Botham, not everyone's idea of an after-dinner speaker, had some pretty forceful points to make on his side, too. In the event, the two Ians failed to agree, but Botham came decisively best out of the argument. It was a pity that, when second-hand accounts

of the altercation were heard, there were some people who did
not show Botham's own proud opinion of his country.

The out-argued Chappell, meanwhile, paid restrained tribute
to the young England lion on television at Headingley.

It was supremely ironic, in any case, that Botham himself was
attributing his breakthrough in Test cricket to what he had been
taught in Australia.

He told me: 'I was instructed by Frank Tyson into the
Australian way of bowling. Basically it meant that you don't aim
your delivery at the stumps, but bowl to your slips.'

In Botham's case the advice was the more invaluable because
of the phenomenal swing he manages to achieve, sometimes
even on a cloudless day.

Yet, although the advice has since brought him such
outstanding success, his stay in Melbourne was, in his own
words, 'disastrous'. While the other three on this initial
Whitbread scheme – Mike Gatting (Middlesex) and Yorkshire's
Bill Athey and Graham Stevenson – did well enough, Botham
watched the rain come down day after day.

'It was the wettest summer in Melbourne for years and I'm

the sort of chap who thrives on hard work, so consequently my efforts were disastrous. The club I was playing for finished with the wooden spoon in the local competition, I picked up only a few wickets and my best score was 40 odd. I had a terrible time,' he recalls.

Now, just a few months later, he had scattered the cream of Australian batting twice in his first two Tests. He was able to reflect at Headingley, as Australia were forced to follow on an awesome 333 runs behind: 'I've really surprised them. They'd heard all about my disappointing performances in Melbourne and made it pretty clear they didn't think much of me as a player. That makes it that much sweeter.'

However, although England now went about grinding Aussies' noses in the mud of their own making, and had them in a hopeless position at 120 for four in the second innings before rain and bad light ended play early on the Saturday, Botham's world had soured somewhat despite his figures of five for 21 earlier in the day.

It had nothing to do with his failure to take a further wicket – Tony Greig, in fact, had looked to his laurels and taken the first two Australian second innings wickets – but the pain he was feeling in his left foot.

He was unable to join his team-mates in the Monday celebrations as they mopped up the last six wickets to bring the Ashes back by an emphatic innings and 85 runs, amid ecstatic cheers from the Headingley fans who had paid £140,000 over the four days for the privilege of being present at a great occasion.

To his dismay Botham was told he had fractured a bone in his foot and he could forget about cricket for the rest of the season.

In other circumstances he might have been privately grateful for the chance to put his feet up after all the pressures of an exacting season, but the final month could have meant so much to him.

For one thing, he had his hopes pinned on helping Somerset to the final of the Gillette Cup. Their semi-final match against Middlesex at Lord's, however, was to become the unhappiest event in the history of Gillette ties. Scheduled for 17 August, two days after the fourth Test, it had to be postponed until 18 August because of heavy rain and again until 19 August when it also rained. It was rearranged for 24 August and it rained, for 25 August and it rained and finally, in the most farcical manner, a 15-over thrash was fixed for Friday, 26 August when the only objects which rained down were Somerset wickets as, inviting suicide with every shot, they contrived to be bowled out for 59 in 14·4 overs and were easily beaten by six wickets.

Balcony appearance. Celebrating the return of the Ashes at Headingley, 1977: (*from the left*) Brearley, Willis, Roope, Greig, Ian and Knott.

That was by far from being Botham's biggest disappointment. When he was ordered to end his season early he had a very real chance of that rarity of modern cricket, the double of 1,000 runs and 100 wickets.

The last player to have achieved the feat had been Fred Titmus back in 1967. When Botham was obliged to bow out for the rest of the season he had scored 738 runs (average 30·75) and taken 88 wickets (average 22·53) and, allowing for his automatic selection for the fifth and final Test at The Oval, he would also have had a possible three more Championship matches in which to reach the milestone and, in such buoyant mood, would have been a good bet to make it.

It is ironic that, entirely influenced by the fact that Botham had all but proved the feat could be done even in these concertinaed days of first-class fixtures, the sales incentive company Bonusplan Ltd announced in 1978 a prize of £10,000 to the first player to do it. The money remains on the table.

England
1st innings

Close of play
First Day
England 252–4
Boycott 110 not out
Roope 19 not out

Umpires
W. E. Alley
W. L. Budd

Brearley	c Marsh	b Thomson	0
Boycott	c Chappell	b Pascoe	191
Woolmer	c Chappell	b Thomson	37
Randall	lbw	b Pascoe	20
Greig		b Thomson	43
Roope	c Walters	b Thomson	34
Knott	lbw	b Bright	57
Botham		b Bright	0
Underwood	c Bright	b Pascoe	6
Hendrick	c Robinson	b Pascoe	4
Willis		not out	5
Extras (b 5, lb 9, w 3, nb 22)			39
Total			436

Fall of wickets: 1–0, 2–82, 3–105, 4–201, 5–275, 6–398, 7–398, 8–412, 9–422

Bowling: Thomson 34–7–113–4, Walker 45–21–97–0, Pascoe 34·4–10–91–4, Walters 3–1–5–0, Bright 26–9–66–2, Chappell 10–2–25–0

On the way to a stunning five for 21. The England fielders converge on Ian as Hookes is lbw at Headingley.

August 11, 12, 13, 15

Australia
1st innings

Close of play
Second Day
Australia 67–5
Robinson 6 not out
Marsh 0 not out

McCosker		run out	27
Davis	lbw	b Hendrick	0
Chappell	c Brearley	b Hendrick	4
Hookes	lbw	b Botham	24
Walters	c Hendrick	b Botham	4
Robinson	c Greig	b Hendrick	20
Marsh	c Knott	b Botham	2
Bright		not out	9
Walker	c Knott	b Botham	7
Thomson		b Botham	0
Pascoe		b Hendrick	0
Extras (lb 3, w 1, nb 2)			6
Total			**103**

Fall of wickets: 1–8, 2–26, 3–52, 4–51, 5–66, 6–77, 7–87, 8–100, 9–100
Bowling: Willis 5–0–35–0, Hendrick 15·3–2–41–4, Botham 11–3–21–5

2nd innings

Close of play
Third Day
Australia 120–4
Chappell 29 not out
Robinson 11 not out

McCosker	c Knott	b Greig	12
Davis	c Knott	b Greig	19
Chappell	c Greig	b Willis	36
Hookes	lbw	b Hendrick	21
Walters	lbw	b Woolmer	15
Robinson		b Hendrick	20
Marsh	c Randall	b Hendrick	63
Bright	c Greig	b Hendrick	5
Walker		b Willis	36
Thomson		.b Willis	0
Pascoe		not out	0
Extras (b 1, lb 4, w 4, nb 15)			27
Total			**248**

Fall of wickets: 1–31, 2–35, 3–63, 4–97, 5–150, 6–167, 7–179, 8–244, 9–245
Bowling: Willis 14–7–32–3, Hendrick 22·5–6–54–4, Greig 20–7–64–2, Botham 17–3–47–0, Woolmer 8–4–8–1, Underwood 8–3–16–0

England won by an innings and 85 runs

The Making of Bionic Botham

He was neither born in a trunk, nor found in a handbag, but there was still a certain geographical misjudgment about the birth of Ian Terence Botham on 24 November 1955. He emerged prematurely into the world at an unheralded place called Heswall in Cheshire, with his father not over-happy at the haste of his first born's arrival. But then Ian Botham has always been ahead of his time. A Somerset hero at eighteen, an England Test player at 21, the country's most competitive sportsman before his 23rd birthday. Is there no limit to the lad's precociousness? Probably not.

Leslie Botham's private pique at Ian's birth in a county of such sporting insignificance as Cheshire was locked in the lore of all Yorkshiremen. Their pudding, their Leeds United, their fish and chips may be renowned, but the aim of all Yorkshire fathers is to see their sons wear the white rose on the county's cricket fields.

For Yorkshire will not, of course, allow the wearing of their colours by any boy not born within their boundaries. It is a stubborn tradition dating back to the days when playing for club, county or country was the ultimate honour ahead of any financial gain. Only Yorkshire among seventeen first-class counties still insist on this qualification today and they probably pay for such diehard tradition by their glaring failure to figure among today's trophy winners. They operate at a disadvantage against teams transfused by the talents of overseas stars.

The effect, anyway, was that Ian Botham, as Yorkshire ingrained as could be imaginable, did not qualify for his natural county.

Ian's future, in fact, was shaped before his third birthday when the Botham family moved south to Yeovil in Somerset, and the tough young would-be Tyke, if not picking up the zyder-apple accent, was brought up very much a son of Zummerzet.

It was inevitable that Ian would immediately adopt an enthusiasm for sport. His parents were steeped in the stuff, with

a clear accent on cricket. Dad, who had been a regular in the Fleet Air Arm for twenty years spanning the war, played for the Royal Navy side, while even Mum remembers an occasion at Sherborne when she captained a nursing service team.

Against such a sporting background, Ian was strongly encouraged at school and made the teams at Milford School and Buckler's Mead. Long before his teens it was a common sight to see him, kit at the ready, at the local recreation ground eager to get a game if a side were one short.

His bounding enthusiasm and obvious flair brought him into the various county youth teams and it was as a result of regular attendance at the county club's coaching sessions that Somerset's recommendations – and his own insistence – led eventually to an invitation to join the MCC Ground Staff at Lord's. He did not just rely on recommendations, but used his own persuasion to win his chance.

This hardly surprised Bill Andrews, the Somerset coach, who said: 'At fourteen, Ian was the most promising cricketer I had ever seen. Full of cricket and full of confidence. He even had a bit of a superiority complex, but there was nothing particularly wrong about that.'

Ian was sixteen when he left home for London and Lord's. It

was a Spartan existence to test the most enthusiastic youngster for, from a weekly wage of £10, six pounds went on lodgings and another pound on underground fares. Then there were the jovial jibes of the other ground staff boys about his inability to bowl. 'Even when Somerset first called me back to play in Sunday League games at seventeen and I bowled my eight overs, they still wouldn't have it that I could bowl,' he says.

In any case, how could such an unquenchable spirit be deflated by sly digs and an existence on the breadline? Just how determined he was to make the grade was vividly demonstrated not long after his Lord's arrival when he was offered the chance of signing on for Crystal Palace as a professional footballer. His flair for sport had, of course, not been confined to cricket. He played statutory rugby at school, once won an under-15 county badminton doubles championship and played plenty of football.

Says Ian: 'I was a striker or centre-half (friends say he was a very forceful, physical No 5 which is not hard to imagine) and the Palace manager, who was then Bert Head, made this offer.'

Head, ironically, was of Somerset stock and a centre-half in his day himself. 'Anyway, I didn't think I was good enough and thought I'd make a much better go in cricket. The prospects for a professional footballer of making a lot of money if he really got on in the game didn't come into my thinking. You see, I consider soccer a much more cut-throat profession and, besides, cricket has always been my first love. Unlike soccer, you're both a member of a team and, at the same time, playing as an individual.'

So he continued to learn his chosen trade at Lord's, while building up his already impressive frame on a Somerset building site in the winter. There were several impressive performances in the second eleven, but the big call from his adopted county did not finally come until Sunday, 2 September 1973, when he was selected for Somerset's John Player League match at Hove against Sussex.

It was an unexceptional debut. Ian, battling seventh, was leg before to Buss for two and his three overs cost 22 runs, but he did have the satisfaction of catching the colossus himself, Tony Greig. How could the tall, fair-haired god of English cricket have known as he walked out that the youngster who had just dismissed him would one day – only four years later, in fact – replace him as the country's recognised No 1 all-rounder?

Somerset ended their season the following Sunday at The Oval against Surrey and Botham was again given a game for the experience. Still batting seventh, he was caught and bowled by Intikhab Alam for two again, and his four overs not only yielded fourteen runs but secured his first wicket in top-class company.

Joy unconfined. Ian runs to praise an amazing catch by Viv Richards in the Kent semi-final of 1974. But, once again, his side were to lose at the last gasp.

The victim was Geoff Howarth, trapped leg before, and again how could the New Zealand Test star have then known that their paths were persistently to cross in the future?

Inevitably, Botham was brought on to the Somerset playing staff for the 1974 season and flung straight into the fray for the opening Championship match against Lancashire at Taunton, a traumatic experience as Somerset were denied their first wicket until the Lancashire openers Barry Wood and David Lloyd had both scored centuries and put on an awesome 265.

Somerset, however, gave Botham a 'feel' for the first-class game, keeping him in the side, nursing his bowling stints before the first milestone – his initial first-class wicket at Bristol. He had a young Cornishman called Malcolm Dunstan, now departed from the county scene, leg before. His figures of one for 51 in 14 overs, however, were nothing to talk about, but his mentors persisted with his bowling action.

He says: 'I knew I could bowl, so did Tom Cartwright, one of the greatest medium-pacers in the business. He, Peter Robinson and Ken Palmer (now a noted umpire) helped me a lot. They used to say: "Come on, let's put a bit of effort into it" and in the end it clicked.'

The major moment came, of course, on 12 June that summer when Botham became a hero in the Benson and Hedges Cup defeat of Hampshire and there were to be compelling little

cameos to follow. He hit a quite magnificent 59 against Middlesex, with two soaring sixes, in another Championship match and, at the Weston-super-Mare festival, produced his best bowling by returning five for 59 against Leicestershire and seven wickets in the match.

Study in concentration. A determined Ian in untypically cautious mood during a 1975 county match against Leicester.

This first full season for Somerset coincided with one of the county's most successful years. They finished fifth in the Championship, second in the John Player League after rain had robbed them of the chance of overhauling eventual champions Leicestershire in the penultimate fixture, and were beaten semi-finalists in both the Gillette and Benson and Hedges Cup competitions.

In no way could Botham be said to have been carried along on this crest of success. He played a full part as his final first-class return of 441 runs and 30 wickets demonstrates.

The following season – Somerset's centenary year of 1975 – could have been crucial. The county cricketers' grapevine which passes on the strengths and weaknesses of precocious young newcomers has destroyed the confidence of plenty of players. It hardly helped, either, that Somerset, expecting to enlarge on their successes of 1974, had a particularly disappointing season, never challenging for any of the titles.

Ian freely confesses: 'Talk to any players and they agree that the first year is the easiest. After that opponents start to find out

about you.' Yet he hit 584 runs and took some sixty-two wickets.

Now it was quite clear that an exceptional young talent was in the making and 1976 brought some quite brilliant performances. The only players being found out were the opposition, for early in May he savaged the Sussex attack at Hove with two sixes and thirteen fours in a thrilling innings that sadly ended at 97, as he was bowled essaying a drive. To his great credit, the only response to such bad luck on the brink of a maiden century was a sunny beam at his own bad shot. In any case that first hundred was to come at Trent Bridge – 167 not out to follow a first innings 80 – and an end-of-season 88 that took him to 1,022 runs for the season.

There were wickets galore, as well, eleven in the match against Gloucestershire including six for 25 in sixteen overs. That was to be exceeded at Bournemouth by a quite staggering spell of six wickets for ten runs in nine overs.

The moment of most importance, however, occurred at Taunton against the most powerful West Indian touring team of all time. Somerset, having been hammered for 389 for eight, had subsided to 70 for five when Botham entered and, against the furious pace of Andy Roberts and Wayne Daniel, it did not look as though the match would see its scheduled third day.

Botham, however, with the devil-may-care daring of vibrant youth, then cracked two sixes, nine fours and made 56 of the next 69 runs. At the other end all this time was his captain, Brian Close, who was to go on to 88 and a recall to the England team at the age of 45.

After such raw courage there could be no overlooking him any longer, especially as England had been humiliated in the Test series by West Indies, so, with three one-day internationals to round off the tour, Botham was brought into the England party. He was still several months short of his twenty-first birthday and it was explained that his inclusion in the squad was to give Botham a small taste of the bigtime.

It was hardly a happy week for him. Picked for the first game at Scarborough, Ian was out for only one, hooking defiantly at Michael Holding and his three overs were thrashed for 26 runs, although he did, at least, earn the wicket of Laurence Rowe. Left out of the second game, he came back at Edgbaston and, although making 20, his bowling figures were even more embarrassing. Again he got a wicket, bowling the tailender, Holding, but his three overs on this occasion cost 31 including a six struck clean out of the ground by Gordon Greenidge. 'No mean feat on such a large ground,' recorded Wisden. 'No more than a club cricketer,' acidly commented a member of cricket's ruling body of Botham. But, then, everybody can make mistakes!

The brave baptism. Batting against West Indies at Edgbaston in the second of his two one-day games for England in 1976. Deryck Murray is the 'keeper.

A Winter's Tale

Ian Botham had no real reason to feel frustrated as the fractured bone in his left foot slowly mended at the end of the 1977 season. The medical explanation for his misfortune was that he had been over-bowled during the summer and he had certainly pounded down some 676 overs for a return of 88 for 1,938 in first-class cricket alone. Certainly, too, being forced to miss the final month of the fixture list had deprived him of that 1,000 runs-100 wickets double and an appearance in the final Test at The Oval where, significantly, Australia's batsmen at last salvaged some self-respect with a score of 385 in a drawn match.

Above all that, though, there had been some very happy events, most notable being the birth to his young wife Kathryn of a very bouncing baby son weighing in at an impressive 8lb 9oz. It will be interesting to see whether one Liam James Botham one day plays for England at cricket, because I cannot recall a Liam ever having been beneath an England cap. Whereas it had been his father's foiled intention to see Ian himself born in and therefore useful one day to Yorkshire, young Liam was safely delivered within that noble county's boundaries, to the chagrin of Ian's Somerset admirers.

The next happy event occurred when the Cricket Writers' Club, in the manner of the England Test selectors they so often take to task, belatedly bestowed on Ian the worthwhile accolade Young Cricketer of the Year. For once in a while the writers had, indeed, got it right. A look back through the list in the 1970s reveals a very arguable honours list if taken from hindsight. In 1970, Yorkshire's Chris Old (no complaints about that); 1971 was John Whitehouse (now the Warwickshire captain, but the great White-hope has hardly lived up to those early expectations); 1972's Dudley Owen-Thomas (Surrey) was soon to give up the game, as many Oval members feel a number of Surrey players should do; in 1973 it was Mike Hendrick (not quite a case of Derbyshire whistling down the pits for another pace bowler, since he had joined the electricity board), but his best, because of incessant injury, is yet to come; 1974's Phil

Edmonds (Middlesex) was as worthy as Old; Lancashire's
Andrew Kennedy in 1975 must still wonder why; while
Derbyshire's Geoff Miller (1976) has still to convince a large
proportion of the public that he has better claims than others to a
place in England touring parties, let alone Test teams.

To be fair to fellow writers, however, they had a vintage crop
in the mid-1960s with Boycott, Brearley, Knott, Underwood
and Greig.

The third event confirmed the stature Ian had attained that
past summer. He was named in the England party of sixteen to
tour Pakistan and New Zealand that winter under the leadership
of Brearley with Boycott his right-hand man. The names of the
sixteen assumed greater than usual significance since they were
to represent the reformation, if not the renaissance, of English
cricket in the wake of Kerry Packer.

By the time the party took off gratefully from a clammy English autumn, the Kerry Packer cricket extravaganza in Australia was well under way and England had washed their hands of Greig, Knott, Underwood, Amiss, Woolmer and Snow.

These players had been the backbone of the England team for most of the 1970s and now England were entering the unknown with a bunch of players largely unproven, untested at all or unable over previous years to hold down a regular place.

The sixteen were: Mike Brearley (Middlesex, captain), Geoff Boycott (Yorkshire, vice captain), Ian Botham (Somerset), Geoff Cope (Yorkshire), Paul Downton (Kent), Phil Edmonds (Middlesex), Mike Gatting (Middlesex), Mike Hendrick (Derbyshire), John Lever (Essex), Geoff Miller (Derbyshire), Chris Old (Yorkshire), Derek Randall (Notts), Graham Roope

(Surrey), Brian Rose (Somerset), Bob Taylor (Derbyshire) and Bob Willis (Warwickshire).

Above: Tour party on parade at Lord's before departure. Ian and county captain Brian Rose are together in the back row.

For Botham there was the pleasant prospect of being on tour with his county colleague Brian Rose, who had just recently been named as successor to Brian Close as Somerset captain. Close had retired from the first-class game at the end of the 1977 season, making his announcement most poignantly on the day Ian was taking five for 74 in his Trent Bridge Test debut.

Rose, tall, lean, with typical straw-blond Somerset hair (although he had been born, but not brought up, in Kent) had interrupted his cricket career to complete his teacher training, and had since blossomed (if the pun can be pardoned) into a stylish left-handed opening batsman.

He had been on the verge of the England team all summer and played some superb innings, including an unbeaten 110 in his county's historic win over the Australians, 205 against Northants at Weston-super-Mare and his 60-over 128 in the Gillette Cup tie against Derbyshire at Ilkeston. Brian Close rated him no less highly than Botham; another old Yorkshire stalwart Ray Illingworth thought him the best young opener he had seen in quite a while.

So the Somerset adventurers set off with the rest of the England party in late November 1977. Pakistan, marginally after India, is the least popular tour on the Test itinerary. The

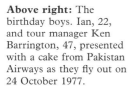

Above right: The birthday boys. Ian, 22, and tour manager Ken Barrington, 47, presented with a cake from Pakistan Airways as they fly out on 24 October 1977.

climate is oppressive, the food very foreign and upsetting to the English digestive organs, and the public excitable to the point where 'Riot stopped play' is as common as our own 'Rain stopped play'. In the political situation of 1977-78, with the former President Bhutto languishing in gaol and the military in command, it was a potentially turbulent place to be.

For a bowler like Botham there was also the hardship of having to toil away on totally unresponsive, hard, mud-rolled wickets. Clearly, England would have to pack their Test side with spinners; only a freak of fortune was likely to bring Botham much success.

Batting on such pitches also presented a problem to his naturally aggressive style. The ball would come slowly on to the bat and make forcing shots the rarity rather than the rule, the scoring of runs the reward for hard graft. To a batsman of Boycott's temperament and technique this represented a challenge to be relished, but it was not Botham's game at all.

Just to increase Botham's burden, there were only nine days of competitive cricket scheduled before the first Test in Lahore.

He was omitted from the opening fixture in Rawalpindi, but played in the following games at Faisalabad and Peshawar and both confirmed his fears that there would be no exciting extravagances for him in this demanding country.

In the first game at Faisalabad he was happy enough to watch

Rose hit an unbeaten 110 as England totalled 284 for one against a United Bank XI, with Boycott lovingly accumulating 123 not out at the other end. Brearley thoughtfully pushed Botham up the order in the second innings when the match was meandering to a draw, but he got a duck. As for his bowling, a combined analysis of one for 46 in 16 eight-ball overs was economical and also unremarkable.

At Peshawar against the Governor's XI, England enjoyed that peculiarity to Pakistan cricket – an actual result. They won by 212 runs, the only first-class fixture of the tour that was not to be drawn, but Botham's part was minor – 22 not out and none for 23 in only eight overs.

He had to be content, therefore, with passing a few pleasantries over the air to the Radio 3 audience back home as his contribution to the first Test, which was dead from the neck

A completely different world. The sights peculiar to Pakistan cricket: (*above*) pitch invaders return to their seats and (*right*) preparing the Karachi Test pitch!

up long before Pakistan deigned to declare their first innings well into the third day.

There was a bit of fun to be had two days before Christmas when the situation in the first of three one-day internationals in Sahiwal tasted a little like home. He went to the wicket with England needing 28 to win and in a hit-or-miss finish found himself facing the last ball with the scores tied at 208. In the true Botham tradition he cracked the left-arm Liaquat Ali through the cover cordon to clinch victory.

He also hit the winning run, although not under such exciting circumstances, in the second one-day international at Sialkot, but for a cricketer who has always wanted to be in the action, whether bowling, batting or fielding, those winter days far from home were sheer frustration.

Only Boycott could genuinely have enjoyed this half of the tour in the cricketing sense. He finished the series of Tests – all of which were drearily predictable draws – with an average of 82·25. Much more important, he had assumed his lifelong ambition of captaining his country when Brearley broke his arm and had to fly home soon after the second Test.

The only cloud on his horizon was centred on Australia, where Greig had accused Boycott in recent years of deliberately avoiding confrontation with the world's fastest bowlers. The Packer empire was again in the news when Pakistan sent for Packer players to join their team for the last Test. These events led the England camp to hold a critical meeting and threaten to strike rather than play against Packer men.

Mushtaq Mohammad, Zaheer Abbas and Imran Khan had flown in to Karachi from Australia, but, under the strong stand the England party had taken, with Botham a particularly

forceful opponent of a Packerstan, the home country's resolve was broken and back flew Mushtaq, Zaheer and Imran to Australia from their fool's errand.

As far as this part of the tour had been concerned, Pakistan had been something of a fool's errand also for Botham, but the entire party were more than happy to fly on to the second half of the tour in the last week of January 1978.

For all the frustrations, they had been bonded together by Brearley into a happy band, and had come out of the three-Test series unbeaten, thus confounding those critics who had thought Pakistan might severely maul this untried team. Boycott was fortunate, indeed, to have inherited such a contented crew.

In fairness also to the Pakistan authorities, who had tried to be as hospitable as possible in unhelpful circumstances, there were such instances of consideration as the £100 pushed into the pocket of Brian Rose shortly before their departure to cover cash that had been stolen from his hotel bedroom.

New Zealand was to be an altogether different proposition from Pakistan. The climate, conditions, people, food, accommodation were as akin to England as they could have wished.

This New Zealand tour was also something of a novelty. England in the past had normally paid patronising recognition to the islands' cricketing aspirations by fitting in a couple of Tests at the end of tours to Australia. These were treated as a bit of a chore and bore by players anxious to be on their way home after the long and arduous Australian tour. That New Zealand had never beaten England added to the lack of any sense of occasion.

This time, however, attitudes had altered. The England party

were actually pleased to be there. They were still proving themselves at Test level and the series would be a keenly-contested three-match rubber and not, as in the past, a mere question of showing the MCC flag in its farthest-flung outpost.

The warm-up match was against Auckland and, ironically, Botham again watched his county colleague Rose score a century, while he himself made 33 and had the unexceptional bowling figures of one for 63.

A one-day up-country game followed before Botham was rested from a remarkable match at New Plymouth in which Central Districts, from an apparently winning position, were bowled out with the scores tied.

Botham generated his own excitement against Canterbury at Christchurch in the following match, a curtain-raiser to the first Test. Having been dismissed for a duck first time round and

then returning his best bowling analysis of the tour to date – 11–3–28–3 – his powerful batting was at last seen at its devastating best for the first time in an England game.

That the match was headed for a draw made no difference to his exciting assault on an attack containing four New Zealand Test bowlers including the rapidly improving Richard Hadlee, son of the former Kiwi captain Walter Hadlee. Young Richard had emphasised his importance and forewarned England with a first innings return of 5 for 50. He was very quick and very hostile and very raw. He recognised in Botham a kindred type of cricketer, perhaps, and tried to soften him up with bouncers. Ian recalls: 'Yes, he bounced me a few times and I successfully hooked him a few times. "That's that and give me another!" I would call out to him.'

Hadlee, still too inexperienced to see through it all, would respond with wilder and wilder deliveries and by the time England declared their second innings at 230 for four, Botham had blazed his way to a thrillingly entertaining 126 not out with a six and some eighteen fours. If Botham was in buoyant mood back at the team's hotel that night, Hadlee was scowling and anxious to settle scores when the first Test started at Wellington in three days' time. And how he did!

The tied match against Central Districts had served as a warning that this Test series was to be like no other England had experienced in New Zealand, and on a rain-affected first day the Kiwi resolution was revealed in a total of 152 for three.

John Wright, a tall, lean left-handed opener who played by the textbook and who had headed the batting averages in his first season for Derbyshire the previous summer, batted through for 55, but Botham had him leg before without a run added next day.

New Zealand advanced unconcerned to 191 and then crumbled dramatically to 228 all out. Botham, in fact, ended the innings, bowling the spinner Boock to finish with two for 27, but the honours went to the other medium-pacer Old, who took six for 54.

Again New Zealand appeared to have entered the match in an optimistic attitude above their station and, with Boycott in obdurate mood and Roope a reliable partner, England gradually established a strong position. By midway through the third day they had reached 183 for four.

It was then that Hadlee suddenly popped up, as if from a puff of smoke, to play demon king. Roope went, edging as he fended frantically and now Hadlee had Botham to bowl at, his score to settle. If they were kindred cricketing souls, then Botham, too, was every bit as raw as Hadlee in the tactical sense.

Ian takes up the sorry tale: 'He glared at me, put a bloke halfway back to the square leg boundary and bounced me. I took the bait hook, line, sinker and half the rod, stupidly tried to hook him and got caught.'

Hadlee finished with four wickets and England, incredibly, collapsed to 215 all out. Worse, far worse, was to follow.

On a wearing wicket Bob Willis wreaked havoc, taking five for 13 as New Zealand tottered to 123, Botham himself returning two for 13 in nine overs, and England were left only 137 to win.

The Wellington wicket was now well worn but that, it was widely agreed, was not an adequate excuse for the way England shouldered arms and surrendered. By the close of the fourth day they had crashed to 53 for eight and the end was delayed by only another eleven runs next morning. New Zealand, by 72 runs, had beaten England for the first time after 50 years. Hadlee was the hero. He had taken six for 24 in the second innings, which hoisted his match figures to a magnificent ten for 100.

That Botham had top-scored in England's second innings with 19 he does not rate among his souvenirs, especially as he had again been one of Hadlee's victims. The reaction at home was wholly predictable, with all the gloomy forebodings of doom voiced about this inexperienced, untried England team allegedly come home to roost. Poor Boycott, poor selectors, poor England. The critics and cartoonists were in their element; for once Tony Greig's comments from across the Tasman Sea were unrecorded and unwanted.

When, within an hour of the start of the second Test at Christchurch nine days later, England, after winning the toss, had lost their first three batsmen, Boycott included, for 26, it seemed there was to be no end to their embarrassment.

Roope, with Miller, who later had to retire hurt, set about restoring the situation, but with the fourth and fifth wickets falling at 127 and 128, England again seemed destined for a depressingly inadequate total. In such unpromising circumstances and with all the front-line batsmen back in the hutch, Botham went to the crease. He was quickly joined by Taylor and together they saw a critical situation through until stumps and 172 for five. Botham, applying a defensive technique totally alien to his nature, was 22 not out; Taylor, with a tailor-made style to suit requirements, on 18; and Hadlee, having taken three wickets and thirsting for more, quite unable to tempt Botham this time.

The following day was a fascinating duel of wits. While Taylor pushed and prodded, Botham accumulated, sensibly picking the balls to hit and confounding all who expected the sudden impatient swipe that had always impaired his approach.

They were still together at lunch and carried on without alarm deep into the afternoon. Botham was scoring two to one against Taylor and slowly and surely his maiden Test century hove into sight . . . as Taylor approached his maiden Test fifty.

They had been together almost five hours when Botham reached 99 and, showing nerves in the nineties for the only time in his career, he shouted suicidally for a single which was never there. Taylor was left as the sacrificial offering.

The little Derbyshire wicketkeeper, always considered technically superior to Knott behind the stumps but given one token Test in his career (on an earlier New Zealand tour)

Touching their new hero. Acclaim from the Christchurch fans on completion of a maiden Test century.

because of the Kent man's oft-proven batting ability, had made 45. More important, this supposedly insufficient batsman had helped Botham add 160 runs to transform totally England's immediate outlook.

Botham, unperturbed, surely arrived at his century and, as so often occurs after a long stand, was out as well five runs later, caught behind trying to attack Boock's spin. He had gone in at 127 for four, he walked out five hours and eleven minutes later at 293 for seven. His 103 had included twelve fours and a six, not a big percentage of boundaries by his hard-hitting standards, but he had shown a sense of responsibility in his restrained batting that suggested he had come of age as a cricketer.

England eventually totalled an unbeatable 418 with the unlucky Miller again denied his own maiden century in any match. He had been left high and dry on 98 in Lahore; in Christchurch, having returned to the crease after injury, he was out for 89.

Botham, meanwhile, had he been like most mortals, would have been tempted to relax, if not rest, on his laurels, but, as was becoming already so evident, he strives for action all the time he is on the field.

The way in which he continued to attract the attention of the Christchurch crowd, however, was not to his liking or theirs. Edmonds and Willis had already broken through, but opener Anderson was going extremely well with 62 of a total of 82 for two when Edmonds ended his resistance with a ball which bowled him round his legs.

The New Zealand crowd, never in the past so raucous as their cousins across in Australia, but now emboldened by the first Test triumph, started booing and it became obvious that their target was Botham and the unfair footmarks he was making on his follow-through. It was one of these, they claimed, that had caused Anderson's downfall and the boos became chants of 'cheats' as skipper Mark Burgess, who was batting at the other end, fuelled a fiery situation by pointedly walking across to his opposite number and nodding in the direction of the crease as he conferred with Boycott.

The Christchurch crowd were soon to discover that baiting Botham creates the opposite effect from that desired. It only increases his resolve, if that were possible, and although the umpires did, indeed, respond by issuing an official warning, the last major event of this third day was the dismissal of the old New Zealand warhorse Bev Congdon, lbw to Botham, of course.

He resumed after a rest day he would happily have done without by breaking right through New Zealand's batting. Burgess he had held by that safest of slip catchers, Roope, the

Acrobatics from Geoff Miller remove Warren Lees, and Ian is on the way to his 8-wicket haul at Christchurch.

wicketkeeper Lees timorously touched him to Miller's hands and, after resistance from Parker, Botham came back to collect the wickets of Collinge and Chatfield and finish with 24·7–6–73–5. For the third time in four Tests he had taken five wickets in an innings, but his contribution to the match was still very far from complete.

New Zealand, 235 all out, had escaped the follow-on by sixteen runs and Boycott, with a positive approach he so rarely showed in Yorkshire, ordered his batsmen to get a move on for the rest of the fourth day. If they were to press home their lead of 183 and have a chance of squaring the series, England needed an early declaration on the last day.

The hectic pursuit of runs which followed had, however, no connection with the running out of Randall. Boycott was batting at the other end but, unlike his Trent Bridge comeback the previous summer, he had no part of Randall's dismissal.

The spinner Chatfield ran up to bowl at Boycott and, without warning, whipped off the bails as Randall started backing up and startled umpire Fred Goodall was obliged to give him out. It was an unforgiveable act of bad sportsmanship and Burgess did not improve the acrimony that had crept into the series with the trite remark that 'not many batsman put themselves in that position'. He could have added that not many bowlers would stoop to so low a trick, being mindful of the fact that if a batsman is annoying them by backing up too early, the appropriate course of action is to halt in the delivery stride and hold the ball over the bails as a polite warning not to do so again.

Randall, however, had to go, Botham was promoted to No 4 in the order with the purpose of peppering up the scoring rate and in next to no time Boycott, too, was run out. This, though, was a conventional dismissal and the cause of a great deal of dressing room merriment – 'I did it on purpose,' joked Ian – for Boycott has probably no peer since Denis Compton as a batsman of whom to beware when it comes to the calling of a run. In the uncanny way in which they appear to upstage each other, Botham seemed now to be trying to steal that dubious distinction from Boycott. Not that it unduly bothered Botham for, ordered to attack, he revelled in his commission, laying about the bowling for 30 runs in the 36 balls he faced before England closed at 96 for four.

Boycott now had a lead of 279 and he immediately declared in the morning. His faith in his fast bowlers was at once justified as Willis produced a staggering spell of four for nine, and the forced retirement of Burgess to a blow on the elbow. New Zealand were 25 for five and in terrible trouble.

Botham, at this stage in the slaughter, had contributed a

The Second Test Christchurch

England
1st innings

Close of play
First Day
England 172–5
Botham 22 not out
Taylor 18 not out
Miller 31 retired hurt

Second Day
England 394–9
Miller 66 not out
Willis 5 not out

Rose	c Howarth	b Chatfield	11
Boycott	lbw	b Collinge	8
Randall	c Burgess	b Hadlee	0
Roope	c Burgess	b Hadlee	50
Miller	c Congdon	b Collinge	89
Radley	c Lees	b Hadlee	15
Botham	c Lees	b Boock	103
Taylor		run out	45
Old		b Hadlee	8
Edmonds	c Lees	b Collinge	50
Willis		not out	6
Extras (b 14, lb 9, nb 10)			33
Total			**418**

Fall of wickets: 1–15, 2–18, 3–26, 4–127, 5–128, 6–288, 7–293, 8–305, 9–375
Bowling: Hadlee 43–10–147–4, Collinge 26·5–6–89–3, Chatfield 37–6–94–1, Congdon 18–11–14–0, Boock 21–11–41–1

2nd innings

Close of play
Fourth Day
England 96–4
Botham 30 not out
Roope 9 not out

Rose	c Lees	b Collinge	7
Boycott		run out	26
Randall		run out	13
Botham		not out	30
Old		b Collinge	1
Roope		not out	9
Miller			
Radley			
Taylor			
Edmonds			
Willis			
Extras (b 4, lb 3, nb 3)			10
Total	(4 wickets dec)		**96**

Fall of wickets: 1–25, 2–47, 3–67, 4–74
Bowling: Hadlee 6–1–17–0, Collinge 9–2–29–2, Chatfield 5–0–22–0, Congdon 2–0–18–0

February 24, 25, 26, 28 March 1

New Zealand
1st innings

Close of play
Third Day
New Zealand 122–4
Burgess 16 not out
Parker 0 not out

Wright		c and b Edmonds	4
Anderson		b Edmonds	62
Howarth	c Edmonds	b Willis	5
Burgess	c Roope	b Botham	29
Congdon	lbw	b Botham	20
Parker		not out	53
Lees	c Miller	b Botham	0
Hadlee		b Edmonds	1
Collinge	c Edmonds	b Botham	32
Boock	c Taylor	b Edmonds	2
Chatfield	c Edmonds	b Botham	3
Extras (b 4, lb 1, nb 19)			24
Total			**235**

Fall of wickets: 1–37, 2–52, 3–82, 4–119, 5–145, 6–151, 7–153, 8–211, 9–216
Bowling: Willis 20–5–45–1, Old 14–4–55–0, Botham 24·7–6–73–5, Edmonds 34–11–38–4

2nd innings

Target 280

Wright	c Roope	b Willis	0
Anderson		b Willis	15
Howarth	c Edmonds	b Old	1
Burgess		not out	6
Congdon	c Botham	b Willis	0
Parker	c Botham	b Edmonds	16
Lees		b Willis	0
Hadlee	c Botham	b Edmonds	39
Collinge	c Miller	b Botham	0
Boock	c Taylor	b Botham	0
Chatfield	lbw	b Botham	6
Extras (lb 6, nb 16)			22
Total			**105**

Fall of wickets: 1–2, 2–14, 3–19, 4–25, 5–25, 6–59, 7–81, 8–90, 9–95
Bowling: Willis 7–2–14–4, Old 7–4–9–1, Botham 7–1–36–3, Edmonds 6–2–22–2

England won by 174 runs

One of the stunning catches that, with his 103 and 8 wickets, turned the Christchurch Test into a complete personal triumph.

stunning, diving third slip catch to send back Congdon, and the lightning left-handed pick-up to account a little later for Parker at backward leg was almost as spectacular.

All the time Hadlee was offering lone resistance at the other end and he, at least, had some satisfaction while the rest of his side were being scuttled. Botham gleefully bounced him first ball and recalls: 'He got his glove and bat handle up in front of his face just in time. He went through a few different colours. Pretty soon he played this characteristic shot of his, flat-batting a bouncer over the slips for four. I was very annoyed and lost my rag. I bowled badly and he smashed me all over the ground.'

Even the skied catch Hadlee put in his hands at square leg did not assuage his annoyance with himself, but polishing off the last three wickets was a splendid panacea for ruffled pride.

New Zealand were all out for 105, England had won by 174 runs, but the match belonged to Botham. He had scored 103 and 30 not out, he had taken 5 for 73 in the first innings, three for 38 in the second and snapped up three catches, two of them quite brilliant. Rarely in cricket history had so young a player – Botham, after all, was only recently turned 22 – stamped himself so forcibly on a Test match.

By contrast, the last drawn Test which tied a sometimes contentious series at 1–1 was almost anti-climax, not that the new young lion of England saw it that way. At Auckland his own performance simply underscored his status as an all-rounder very rapidly reaching world class.

Overbowled because Old was erroneously omitted on an Auckland wicket which was of no help to spinners, Botham still obliged with five for 109 from thirty-four eight-ball overs and then went out to hit the 53 liveliest runs of an England innings that badly lost its way, being spread from second day to fifth by an unnecessarily drawn-out study in stoicism by the mid-winter replacement for Mike Brearley, Clive Radley, who made 158 and effectively killed the match stone-dead. A century in each innings by New Zealand's Geoff Howarth merely added the coffin nails.

The memory of the series – indeed, of the entire winter tour – remained at Christchurch. Of that amazing virtuoso performance by Botham, the England team manager Ken Barrington spared nothing in his appraisal.

'He learns quickly,' said Barrington. 'That's a great asset. In the Wellington Test he fell into Richard Hadlee's trap and got out hooking. He was very upset, but he thought about what he had done wrong. In the Christchurch Test he not only ducked all Hadlee's bouncers but had time to smile back down the wicket at him.' It was a moment of triumph.

Left: Ian (*back right*) leaps to catch New Zealand's Anderson in the drawn final Test at Auckland. Roope and 'keeper Taylor celebrate.

Below: What the Press felt about Ian's impact on the tour of New Zealand, with Brearley joining in the praise.

Warming to his subject, Barrington continued: 'Ian is the most exciting England prospect I have seen in ten years and the best young all-rounder who has emerged in all the years I have been in cricket.'

Then, quite aware his words would be published in every English newspaper next day: 'I put him in the same category as the great Australian all-rounder Keith Miller.'

And Ian? He flew home via Los Angeles and a special sightseeing visit to Disneyland. It was as if he wanted his dream world to go on forever – as it shows every sign of doing!

DAILY EXPRESS Tuesday March 14 1978

MIKE BREARLEY

Mike Brearley sees a specialist in Birmingham today, hoping for the all clear on his injured arm. He looks healthy enough. Yesterday, the jet-lag had gone and only the New Zealand tan remained. His conclusions on the tour, and forecasts for the summer. . . . Interviewer: Christopher Hilton.

Botham's big time build-up

D. EXP 1 4 III 78

ENGLAND can now face the future with hope and confidence, despite some disappointing results in Pakistan and New Zealand.

Why? Because, very simply, our young all-rounders survived and prospered. They will give us both depth and balance.

Ian Botham, always confident, is now a player of stature and was easily the find of the winter. His bowling is based on attack and he is learning how to build an innings.

He was out hooking in New Zealand in the First Test. In the second, he batted an hour and a half for 19 at a crucial time—and didn't play a single hook.

Phil Edmonds hasn't yet the absolute accuracy of the master bowlers — but he is going that way and fast. His control of length and direction have improved to the point where he had two very good Tests, in Karachi and Christchurch.

And Geoff Miller has matured into a real Test

Botham . . . learning

batsman, to add to his skills as a bowler. Derek Randall However, had a rough time. He became very defensive, trying to sort out his technique.

He has always been a shuffler, but this became more and more pronounced. He was moving so much as the bowler ran up that he ended on or outside off-stump.

So he went to the nets and, hour after hour, worked incredibly hard. Maybe too hard. What he needs now is a month's rest, because Eng-

Botham ton guns down those Kiwis

By February 8 1978

Pat Gibson in Canterbury

...THAM, who loves ...e fields near his ...re home with a ...d New Zealand a blazing salvo ...erday.

...d not realised ...d such artil-...templated a ...pe will give ...Test com-

...awaken-...year-old ...ripped ...s way ...126. ...an-

terbury's 34-year-old opening batsman, Peter Coman, the awakening came in a Christchurch hospital.

It was his misfortune to be in Botham's line of fire at long on where he bravely tried to cling to a searing drive off Bev Congdon.

He failed in the attempt and hit the ground almost at the same time as the ball. He lay motionless for five minutes until being stretchered off.

He was transferred to ...pital where he was deta... with concussion.

The day began with E... land in familiar distress aft... losing three wickets for o... run.

Botham drove, pulled and cut, and an attack containing three of New Zealand's Test squad — Richard Hadlee, Stephen Boock and Congdon —was powerless to contain him.

Dominated

Botham dominated the un... defeated fifth wicket stand of 111 that allowed England to declare at 230 for five.

Just as important was the support he got from wicket keeper Bob Taylor, whose 31 not out was the product of a lot of hard work to improve his batting.

The new ball bowling of Bob Willis and Chris Old put a target of 260 in three and a half hours way out of Canterbury's reach.

The hostile Willis removed Murray Parker and Maurice Ryan at a personal cost of

eight, McEwa... cut hea... bounce... ing for ... who will Test was Hadlee i... wicket ...

The Golden Summer

The cricket season traditionally starts in isolated splendour at Lord's with a match between the county champions and an invited MCC side towards the end of April. The players, swathed in sweaters, may even outnumber those spectators brave enough to watch from without the Long Room, the Press publish the scores, but nobody takes too much notice. As a curtain-raiser it has about as much dramatic appeal as an episode of 'Crossroads'. Or it did until Ian Botham changed all that on 19 April 1978.

A month of shootin' and fishin' (huntin' has not yet figured) and long fitness walks in the Lake District had kept him in trim after the winter tour and, now, on this unfriendly April day he delivered a few looseners, then completely beat and bowled Clive Radley with a lethal break-back which kept low. Next ball Graham Barlow was baffled by a wicked late inswinger which rattled his stumps; and, with a flawless yorker for encore, he bowled Norman Featherstone.

A first-day hat-trick, all bowled, against three most respected Middlesex batsmen was an astonishing feat and an omen if ever there was of what the season held in store for him.

There was the added incentive of financial sponsorship for his exploits from Rank Radio International of Plymouth. It was not now uncommon for star cricketers to enjoy a supplement to their income from such sponsorship – a stamp firm had decided to pay Viv Richards £1 per every run he accumulated in all competitions for Somerset over the next three years; Mike Brearley would motor along on a gallon a run in the summer's Test series – but these bonuses were usually for players in their benefit years or the very top cricketers in the country. At the early age of 22 Ian had joined this elite. The Rank Radio agreement was a remarkable early recognition of his ability. It also made him, if not wealthy, then very well off for his age, especially as, prompted by the Kerry Packer affair, the Cornhill Insurance Company had taken over sponsorship of the Test matches in England, and among their innovations was to increase Test match fees to £1,000. Pakistan and New Zealand, returning the compliment after the winter tour, were both touring during the 1978 summer, which meant six Tests and £6,000 for an ever-present England player, let alone the win bonuses and man-of-the-match awards.

Ian, as mentioned earlier, had as a teenager the opportunity to make a profession of football but, although aware of the potential to make more money, had opted for his first love, cricket. Now, in an atmosphere of increasing hostility to soccer and all its cancerous scandals and sicknesses, more and more sponsors were preferring to plough profits into cricket. Ian's integrity to his first love was paying a handsome profit.

Ian was certainly earning his affluence. The month that followed that first-day hat-trick was full of fine deeds. At Taunton he scuttled Glamorgan with six for 66 in a Schweppes Championship game; against the combined Oxford and Cambridge Benson and Hedges Cup team his four for 16 in eleven overs gave Somerset the title in their qualifying group and earned him the Gold Award; against Gloucestershire, the old rivals, he hit an enthralling 86 and snapped up seven wickets in the match to help Somerset to the top of the Championship. He also allowed his fierce competitiveness to master his commonsense. He had a running battle with the elegant Gloucester and Pakistan batsman Zaheer Abbas, flinging down some furious bouncers for which he was eventually warned. With Zaheer scoring 20 and 140 but both times finally being dismissed by Botham, honours rested about even, but there was little honourable about the way Botham had run out the Gloucestershire opener Alan Tait in the first innings. Tait snicked the ball first bounce to Botham at slip and, turning, saw the ball in the fielder's hands and started walking on the assumption he had been cleanly caught. Botham promptly flung the ball at the stumps and successfully appealed for a run-out. He made enemies over the incident and, with hindsight, wished it had not happened. However, it is hard, in the heat of a moment, to constrain so fiercely competitive a spirit.

There had been a classic precedent four years earlier in the potentially explosive atmosphere of Port of Spain when Tony Greig, Botham's predecessor as England's premier all-rounder, almost triggered a riot by running out Alvin Kallicharran. He had left his crease to start walking to the pavilion under the assumption that play had ended for the day, his partner Bernard Julien having pushed the final ball to Greig at silly point. On that occasion – a Test Match – the umpire's correct decision that he was run out was over-ruled and Kallicharran continued batting next day as tempers were smoothed out.

It was not so with Gloucester's Alan Tait, but, in defence of Ian's unsporting action, it is undeniable that both he and Greig possess that blind dedication to winning which can, on occasion, call into question their judgment. Whatever the mitigating circumstances of that situation, Pakistan, at least, were forewarned that Botham was working himself into aggressive mood for the Test series ahead. They had, of course, no real knowledge of his potential after the frustrating two months he had spent in Pakistan the previous winter, and the two one-day internationals at Old Trafford and The Oval were, by their nature, no indicator, either. England, incidentally, won both games by large margins and the Tourists' build-up to the Tests had been hampered by the most abysmal weather which had led to five of their first six county matches being abandoned.

As badly weakened as any country by the mass defections to

Take that! A Herculean hook off Sikandar Bakht in the century made at Edgbaston in the first Test against Pakistan.

Kerry Packer, the Pakistanis had a sobering opening day in the first Test at Edgbaston. Botham it was who made the breakthrough, taking an agile caught and bowled chance from Mudassar Nazar. Thereafter, the day belonged to Chris Old and when their last wicket fell at 164 on the second morning, he had taken seven for 50, including four wickets in five balls.

England then piled up the runs against a poor attack, further weakened by injury to their one top-class bowler Sarfraz Nawaz. Radley made a century in circumstances much removed from his funereal 158 at Auckland; David Gower, who at 21 years and two months was even younger than Botham had been on his Test debut the previous summer, produced a dazzling little innings of 58.

When Botham at last went to the wicket on Saturday morning, England were already 276 for five, the little Pakistani fielders a

And that! Now Mudassar Nazar gets the treatment. Geoff Miller is the admiring batsman in a 122-stand.

Slaughter of the
innocents: Iqbal Qasim is
caned (*left*); the magic
moment as the first Test
century is achieved (*right*);
and home and dry as
Pakistan skipper Wasim
Bari attempts a run-out
(*below*).

straggle of limp rag dolls and Botham destroyed them. Cover drives leapt from his bat like stones from a sling, the sheer force of his shots entranced an Edgbaston crowd who had not seen this sort of power batting since the days of Ted Dexter. There was never a pause as he pummelled his way to 100. Only then did he consider the job done, holed out without addition and departed to a vast ovation.

England declared at 452 for eight and, although there was early resistance, Pakistan eventually toppled from 196 for two to 231 all out. They had been beaten by an innings and 57 runs.

For Botham there was no brief interlude before the second Test. Somerset, a young and enormously talented side whether with Botham or without, were making fine strides in all competitions which meant that there was no such thing as an 'easy' match. He took his batting from Edgbaston to Bath and a Sunday slog of 52 as he and Richards raked a Lancashire attack for 118 in only sixteen overs; his booming self-confidence became apparent again at Hove in a Benson and Hedges Cup quarter-final where his side were creaking at 24 for three with even Richards out for a duck. Botham then batted as if he had never heard of Hove's notorious morning movement and flayed 54 runs in 45 minutes with eleven fours. Somerset were hoisted to 218, Sussex subsided to 116 and Botham gained a second successive Gold Award.

And so to Lord's and his first England appearance at the headquarters of cricket. This gracious ground may be dwarfed by some of the stadia of Australia and India, but it has a majesty all its own, which has had the effect of unnerving even the greatest of batsmen on the long, lonely walk out to the middle. This, therefore, would be the biggest test yet of Botham's character, and England's fortunes, after the first day had been washed out, put extra pressure upon him.

Brearley and Radley, on their home ground, were gone before the scoreboard registered 20, Gower (again) and Gooch retrieved the situation in a stand of 101 and then England lurched again to 134 for five as the spin of Iqbal Qasim began to bite.

The young lion's answer to that was to loft the second ball he received, also from Iqbal, into the Mound Stand for six! Wisden does not detail such evidence, but it is doubtful whether there have been many batsmen in history who have shown such audacious irreverence on the occasion of their first Lord's Test. And the crowd loved him for it.

All through the afternoon he treated them to the same fearsome hitting that had so electrified the Edgbaston patrons only a fortnight earlier. The Pakistanis were quite powerless to prevent the cascade of shots, some superbly executed, some utterly unorthodox, that flowed from his bat. He was fast approaching a second successive Test century, but with only ten minutes until the close and his score still in the late eighties it seemed to the crowd that he would settle for morning glory. Not Botham. A crowd had come to be entertained and in a quite reckless race with the hands of the clock he hit out until, with the time almost 6.30 pm, he clumped another shot through mid-wicket. Two fielders tore along the boundary from opposite directions, but the ball beat them both and bumped into the boundary boards . . . 102 not out.

Lord's was packed for more on Saturday morning, but after another booming four – his twelfth – to mid-off, he again tried to force the bowler and dragged the ball onto the stumps. He had made 108 of the 190 added while he had been at the wicket.

Poor Pakistan were so demoralised when they at last went in that, by mid-afternoon, they were following on again after being

Study in self-disgust. The lordly Lord's century ends as Ian drags Liaqat Ali into his stumps.

bowled out for 105. At least by the end of the day they had made some semblance of a struggle second time round with a score of 96 for two. Botham, for once, had taken a back seat during the day as Willis (five for 47) and Edmonds (four for six) disposed of the Pakistan first innings, but winners take all so it was hardly surprising that when the England players patronised a Brearley benefit year golf competition in North London on their Sunday of rest it was Botham who walked off with first prize. 'It's pathetic,' he says, 'even when playing games with our baby son I still have to win!'

It was back to cricket on Monday morning with no apparent reason why Pakistan should not prolong the struggle. The sky was cloudless, the spinners expecting to be employed for a long period prising out the Pakistanis and the overnight pair, Mohsin Khan and Talat Ali, had already put on 51 without any major alarms. In the event, after bowling an over from the Nursery End, Willis decided to switch ends and take advantage of the fact that the wind had changed direction. He immediately induced an edge from a lifting ball to Mohsin.

The switch by Willis, meanwhile, had meant someone filling in at the Nursery End to accommodate the odd over. Botham

Left: Thar he goes! First of eight victims in the Lord's Test: Mudassar Nazar edges to Bob Taylor. Mohsin, umpire David Constant and Mike Brearley have the best views.

Below: Now it's Haroon Rashid's turn. Note the horizontal stump. Roope, Brearley, and Taylor cannot believe it.

recalls: 'Mike Brearley could have thrown the ball to Phil Edmonds or Geoff Miller who, after all, were expecting to do a lot of bowling in the day.' Instead he tossed it to Botham who immediately found, by some atmospheric freak, that he could swing the ball to a devastating degree. 'Suddenly in that hot, muggy atmosphere it all happened,' he says. 'The killer ball turned out to be my natural delivery – the outswinger. But the one that had 'keeper Bob Taylor leaping about on the legside was my inswinger and the swing was so great in those conditions I just couldn't control it. One inswinger even went for four wides.

'When I had taken the ball I thought it was for one over, but after a couple there was no way I was going to throw it back.'

Three or four outswingers an over were beating the bat, Brearley himself said afterwards that even if the opposition had been the West Indians or Australia he would have been disappointed not to take four or five wickets that morning. The underprivileged Pakistan batsmen were utterly out of their depth. Talat Ali went to outswing, Haroon Rashid was bowled by inswing, Wasim Raja was conventionally caught and bowled, Wasim Bari edged to Taylor, Sikandar to slip, Qasim's stumps were uprooted by inswing, finally Miandad, who had gallantly

Below left: The smile of success. After the Lord's one-man show.

Below: Even *The Times* forgets its reserve in a show of spontaneous applause as Fleet Street hails a new hero.

held one end for 80 minutes, slashed to gully and Pakistan were all out for 139, beaten by an innings and 120 runs and there were still some seven minutes to spare until lunch.

Botham, having reeled off the last seven wickets to add to the one he took on Saturday, had the quite awesome morning analysis of seven for 14 in 13·5 overs. As the writers reached for Wisden the discovery was made that his innings figures of eight for 34 were the best by an England bowler since Jim Laker's nine for 37 and ten for 53 against Australia at Old Trafford in 1956. Furthermore, Botham's 108 and eight for 34 was unmatched in the annals of all Test cricket. Only Gary Sobers and Mushtaq Mohammad, with a century and five wickets in an innings, came remotely close by comparison.

There was something reverential in the writing of the staid *Daily Telegraph* next day: 'In the past Test selectors have been profoundly grateful for all-rounders who have been worth their place in one department and have performed usefully in the other.

'Ian Botham has played in seven Test matches. He has made three hundreds and a 50 and has taken five wickets or more in an innings five times. And he is only 22.' Heavy words indeed.

The inevitable Man of the Match award from an almost awed Brearley. Ian had just added 8–34 to his 108.

The Second Test Lord's

England
1st innings

Close of play
First Day
No play – Rain

Second Day
England 309–8
Botham 102 not out
Edmonds 6 not out

Umpires
W. L. Budd
D. J. Constant

Brearley	lbw		b Liaqat Ali	2
Gooch	lbw		b Wasim Raja	54
Radley	c Mohsin Khan		b Liaqat Ali	8
Gower			b Iqbal Qasim	56
Roope	c Mohsin Khan		b Iqbal Qasim	69
Miller	c Javed Miandad		b Iqbal Qasim	0
Botham			b Liaqat Ali	108
Taylor	c Mudassar Nazar		b Sikandar Bakht	10
Old	c Mohsin Khan		b Sikandar Bakht	0
Edmonds			not out	36
Willis			b Mudassar Nazar	18
Extras (lb 2, nb 1)				3
Total				**364**

Fall of wickets: 1–5, 2–19, 3–120, 4–120, 5–134, 6–252, 7–290, 8–290, 9–324

Bowling: Sikandar Bakht 21–3–115–2, Liaqat Ali 18–1–80–3, Mudassar Nazar 4·2–0–16–1, Iqbal Qasim 30–5–101–3, Wasim Raja 12–3–49–1

Acclaim for a superman effort. Miller, Edmonds and Gower give Ian an escort of honour after his eight for 34 destroys Pakistan at Lord's.

Pakistan
1st innings

Mudassar Nazar	c Edmonds	b Willis	1
Sadiq Mohammad	c Botham	b Willis	11
Mohsin Khan	c Willis	b Edmonds	31
Haroon Rashid		b Old	15
Javed Miandad	c Taylor	b Willis	0
Wasim Raja		b Edmonds	28
Talat Ali	c Radley	b Edmonds	2
Wasim Bari	c Brearley	b Willis	0
Iqbal Qasim		b Willis	0
Sikandar Bakht	c Brearley	b Edmonds	4
Liaqat Ali		not out	4
Extras (nb 9)			9
Total			**105**

Fall of wickets: 1–11, 2–22, 3–40, 4–41, 5–84, 6–96, 7–97, 8–97, 9–97

Bowling: Willis 13–1–47–5, Old 10–3–26–1, Botham 5–2–17–0, Edmonds 8–6–6–4

2nd innings

Close of play
Third Day
Pakistan 96–2
Mohsin Khan 45 not out
Talat Ali 36 not out

Mudassar Nazar	c Taylor	b Botham	10
Sadiq Mohammad	c Taylor	b Willis	0
Mohsin Khan	c Roope	b Willis	46
Talat Ali	c Roope	b Botham	40
Haroon Rashid		b Botham	4
Javed Miandad	c Gooch	b Botham	22
Wasim Raja		c and b Botham	1
Wasim Bari	c Taylor	b Botham	2
Sikandar Bakht	c Roope	b Botham	1
Iqbal Qasim		b Botham	0
Liaqat Ali		not out	0
Extras			13
Total			**139**

Fall of wickets: 1–1, 2–45, 3–100, 4–105, 5–114, 6–119, 7–121, 8–130, 9–130

Bowling: Willis 10–2–26–2, Old 15–4–36–0, Botham 20·5–8–34–8, Edmonds 12–4–21–0, Miller 9–3–9–0

England won by an innings and 120 runs

The final Pakistan Test was pure anti-climax, with the summer's appalling weather bringing about an abandonment, although Botham, demonstrating his determination to remain walking on water, had a four for 59 return. There were other rich pickings, including a county-best seven for 61 (seven for 28 in the final 15 overs that mattered) at Cardiff before the New Zealand section of the summer took preference.

New Zealand, it soon became clear, although only marginally altered from the side which had squared a series with England the previous winter, were not so formidable in these unfriendly conditions. The first Test at The Oval drifted away from them as they fell headlong to 113 for seven in their second innings.

England eventually wrapped up matters by seven wickets despite losing the fourth day to yet more rain, then amassed 429 in the second Test at Trent Bridge, Boycott hitting an inevitable 131 on his belated return to the team after having missed the previous Pakistan series through a hand injury.

Botham, now burdened by the small boys' expectation of a miracle a match and the older heads who predicted a fall, had been unspectacular by his own high standards at The Oval with only four wickets and an unremarkable 22. But Trent Bridge was like being back home. It was here that he had made his Test debut only a year ago, taken five Australian wickets and been complimented by The Queen. It was here also that he had struck his maiden century in first-class cricket in 1976, a magnificent affair of 167 not out against Nottinghamshire, when he had won a 230-minute chase to score 301 with seven overs to spare by smiting six sixes and twenty fours.

So now Horatio was back astride his Bridge again and, in the hour before the close of the second day, had accounted for both openers and also left the resolute Howarth nursing a headache brought about by a bumper.

As so often in this one-sided summer, a Test match Saturday became a funeral march for the Tourists and once again the last rites were conducted by Botham. From their overnight 35 for three, New Zealand tumbled to 120 all out as Botham unerringly picked them off with his deadly swinging deliveries.

Brearley could well contemplate that captaining England had become ridiculously easy. He had but to bring on Botham, reinforce his slip fielders and simply wait for the catches to come. It happened again now as Botham reeled off another remarkable analysis – 21–9–34–6.

Rain, as it also had done on several Test Saturdays this summer, then ensured the match went into Monday, but the Cornhill Insurance cashier had the Man of the Match cheque yet again made payable to Botham long before the end. There

were two catches this time, a caught and bowled and an inevitable touch to Taylor, as New Zealand quietly conceded defeat by an innings and 119 runs. Botham, returning three for 59, finished the Test with a match aggregate of nine for 93.

And so again to Lord's. The achievements all summer of Botham, let alone that one-man extravaganza at headquarters two months earlier, ensured that even if another series was dead, there was enough enthusiasm for the Somerset demon to ensure that the ground was fairly well filled, Botham by now having become pure box-office. He did not let the patrons down, breaking the opening stand at 65, but for once a touring team showed some fight.

Howarth, without whom the series would surely have fallen apart, batted most determinedly with solid support from his captain, Burgess, and as the end of the opening day approached

Caught in the act! Mike Hendrick salutes the dismissal of Geoff Howarth at Trent Bridge, in the second Test *v* New Zealand, 1978.

with New Zealand nearing 250 and only three wickets down, that English affection for the underdog was in its element. In the space of six runs Botham, however, put a fresh complexion on the innings. He ended a stand of 130 by having Burgess leg before with one which moved into him and then the groping Congdon, a shadow of the gritty man who had twice held England at bay with scores in the 170s a few years earlier, followed his outswing.

New Zealand ended the day at 280 for five and next morning Botham swiftly snuffed out any fond hopes they entertained of approaching an unloseable 400 by bowling Anderson and, with special satisfaction, inducing Hadlee to snick with the swing.

Superman! Space-age style in a crash helmet, Ian lunges for a sensational catch and New Zealand's Bruce Edgar is on his way at Trent Bridge. (*Left to right*) Hendrick, Taylor, Brearley, Radley and bowler Edmonds look amazed.

Finally and fittingly he added the gallant Howarth to his latest collection, a catch to Taylor leaving the New Zealander with 123 of a total of 339. Botham, for once, had been obliged to work really hard for his reward which was six for 103 in 38 overs.

When England batted, Gower again excelled in a stand of 116 with Radley. At the end of the series he would have scored almost 100 runs more than his nearest rival and but for Botham might well have been England's man of the moment. Ian himself was not needed until Saturday morning and 211 for four, but after a disappointing 21 England's last five wickets folded for only forty runs and New Zealand had the rare luxury of a 50-run first innings advantage and the chance to capitalise.

But a Test match Saturday in 1978 would have seemed empty and out of character unless something bizarre occurred before the end of the day. It did, immediately Willis and Botham opened the attack at 5 pm as New Zealand started their second innings.

Both promptly struck and the statutory Saturday rout was on. By the close New Zealand had been whittled down to a pitiful 37 for seven in 25 overs. Willis had taken four for 10, Botham three for 23 and Monday's business was a mere formality. New Zealand were all out for 67, Botham greedily grabbing the last two wickets to return 18·1–4–39–5 and England got home by seven wickets to take the series 3–0.

The summer had been one long story of England success. Of the six Tests, they had won three by margins of an innings, two by seven wickets, while the other had been abandoned to the elements. In the ordinary course of events, it would have been a most unsatisfactory season in that the opposition just were not up to required standards and England's easy ride had been of benefit to no one. But 1978 was exceptional. It was the English public's first opportunity to assess a completely remodelled team following the banishment of the Kerry Packer defectors

The commonplace of '78! Bob Taylor embraces Ian, and others come to applaud as the Kiwis' John Wright is bowled in the final Lord's Test.

and this and their outstanding success kept the crowds coming through the turnstiles. Gower had been a grand little addition, Boycott had reigned imperiously, Willis, free from injury, was at last revealing what a very fine fast bowler he was, but above all was Ian Botham.

Such is the self-denigration that seems to affect all Englishmen in the discussion of sport to the absurd point that they become apologists for success, that there was a large body of sceptical opinion at the start of the summer which held that Botham's two five-wicket hauls against the Australians in 1977 and his winter achievements in New Zealand had been produced against first, an Aussie team which was unable to give of its best because of the disruptions of the Packer crisis, and second, a New Zealand team that was not top Test class.

In 1978, Botham established beyond argument that a very special cricketer had arrived in the England team. He had made 263 runs including, of course, those couple of centuries and averaged over the six Tests a score of 43·83; he had taken 37 wickets, bowled many more overs than anyone else and enjoyed a striking rate of a wicket every 14·75 runs. He had also become that rarity, a genuine box-office crowd attraction.

Ian runs out his old enemy Richard Hadlee (although the camera tries to deny it) and the Lord's Test is as good as won.

The Third Test Lord's

New Zealand

1st innings

Close of play
First Day
New Zealand 280–5
Howarth 103 not out
Anderson 8 not out

Wright	c Edmonds	b Botham	17
Edgar	c Edmonds	b Emburey	39
Howarth	c Taylor	b Botham	123
Parker	lbw	b Hendrick	14
Burgess	lbw	b Botham	68
Congdon	c Emburey	b Botham	2
Anderson		b Botham	16
Hadlee	c Brearley	b Botham	0
Collinge	c Emburey	b Willis	19
Boock		not out	4
Bracewell	st Taylor	b Emburey	4
Extras (b 4, lb 18, w 4, nb 7)			33
Total			**339**

Fall of wickets: 1–65, 2–70, 3–117, 4–247, 5–253, 6–290, 7–290, 8–321, 9–333

Bowling: Willis 29–9–77–1, Hendrick 28–14–39–1, Botham 38–12–103–6, Edmonds 12–3–19–0, Emburey 26·1–12–39–2, Gooch 10–0–29–0

2nd innings

Close of play
Third Day
New Zealand 37–7
Burgess 8 not out

Umpires
H. D. Bird
B. J. Meyer

Wright		b Botham	12
Edgar		b Botham	4
Anderson	c Taylor	b Willis	1
Parker	c Taylor	b Botham	3
Burgess	c Hendrick	b Botham	14
Congdon	c Taylor	b Willis	3
Boock	c Radley	b Willis	0
Bracewell	c Hendrick	b Willis	0
Howarth		not out	14
Hadlee		run out	5
Collinge		b Botham	0
Extras (lb 3, nb 5)			11
Total			**67**

Fall of wickets: 1–10, 2–14, 3–20, 4–29, 5–33, 6–37, 7–37, 8–43, 9–57

Bowling: Willis 16–8–16–4, Botham 18·1–4–39–5, Emburey 3–2–1–0

England
1st innings

**Close of play
Second Day**
England 175–2
Radley 75 not out
Gower not out

Gooch	c Boock	b Hadlee	2
Boycott	c Hadlee	b Bracewell	24
Radley	c Congdon	b Hadlee	77
Gower	c Wright	b Boock	71
Brearley	c Edgar	b Hadlee	33
Botham	c Edgar	b Collinge	21
Taylor	lbw	b Hadlee	1
Edmonds	c Edgar	b Hadlee	5
Emburey		b Collinge	2
Hendrick		b Bracewell	12
Willis		not out	7
Extras (b 7, lb 5, nb 22)			34
Total			289

Fall of wickets: 1–2, 2–66, 3–180, 4–211, 5–249, 6–255, 7–258, 8–263, 9–274
Bowling: Hadlee 32–9–84–5, Collinge 30–9–58–2, Bracewell 19·3–1–68–2, Boock 25–10–33–1, Congdon 6–1–12–0

2nd innings
Target 118

Gooch		not out	42
Boycott		b Hadlee	4
Radley		b Hadlee	0
Gower	c Congdon	b Bracewell	46
Brearley		not out	8
Botham			
Taylor			
Edmonds			
Emburey			
Hendrick			
Willis			
Extras (lb 3, w 4, nb 11)			18
Total		(3 wickets)	118

Fall of wickets: 1–14, 2–14, 3–84
Bowling: Hadlee 13·5–2–31–2, Collinge 6–1–26–0, Boock 5–1–11–0, Bracewell 6–0–32–1

England won by 7 wickets to take the series 3–0

The
Lost Weekend

Everyone in the West Country was immensely proud of Ian Botham. In an area not noted for much sporting achievement aside of the tennis fraternity from Torquay, the Gloucestershire rugby team and, perhaps, the infrequent international appearances of the Devonian soccer player Trevor Francis, to have an England Test cricketer from Somerset was something to shout about. The county had contributed nobody to the Test team in over ten years apart from the emergency appearances in 1976 of Brian Close, and by no stretch of the imagination could 'D.B.' be classified as good Somerset stock.

There is, however, an unfortunate side effect to an unfashionable county offering up one of its own to the national interest. The heavy demands made by selectors on Botham in a summer of six Tests plus one-day international matches meant that Somerset hardly ever saw him.

With his constant England commitments, there emerged an unfair but definitely detectable antagonism among the locals towards Botham. It was almost as if there existed a mental block between them and the 'local boy made good' – 'he doesn't want to know us now he's in the big-time'.

West Country people tend to be defensive almost to the point of an inferiority complex, an attitude borne possibly of the fact that the area is under-developed and off the beaten track.

At any rate, there was a definite air of disillusionment whenever Botham failed with the bat for Somerset, which was becoming unfortunately often. What hardly helped was the fact that Somerset collectively were having a quite spectacular season and Botham kept coming back from his latest exploits for England and failing to achieve anything remotely comparable for his county.

He had, it is true, played a principal part in their progress to the semi-finals of the Benson and Hedges Cup, winning two Gold Awards in the games against the Combined Universities and Sussex, but the crucial match with Kent, the acknowledged kings of one-day cricket, was an unhappy affair which stretched

over three days, with the weather determining Somerset's eventual defeat by 41 runs.

Rose, ninth out for a brave 48, fittingly fired the only shots of defiance as Somerset went down. Defeat, though a great disappointment, was not a disaster, for at this mid-season stage Somerset were clinging firmly to second place in the Schweppes Championship – they had, indeed, led the table for a week – despite the vast drain on their bowling penetration caused by Botham's continual absences.

That they were eventually to finish fifth, after sustaining an outside title challenge almost to the end, when Botham played in only ten of their 22 matches was quite remarkable. In those few appearances, Botham had bagged 58 wickets, so it is tempting to speculate on where they would have been with Botham more often available.

In one department, however, they had not missed him. His batting had been frankly sub-standard, fourteen innings bringing only 275 runs at an average of 19·64, and that would have been considerably less but for an 86 back in May against Gloucestershire. The locals found it increasingly hard to reconcile such statistics with those dashing centuries for England. That other youngsters like Peter Roebuck and Philip Slocombe were producing scores way beyond expectations only served to exasperate them further.

Previous spread: Brave downfall of a hero. Ian bowled for 80 in the 1978 Gillette Cup final after carrying Somerset on his shoulders.

Above: Taunton and the home of Somerset County Cricket. 1978 was a thrilling season for the crowd.

Botham believes that his bowling was so important to a side not noted for its penetrative powers that his batting became the victim. Be that as it may, Botham has always striven mightily for Somerset and the criticism was ill-considered.

Meanwhile, the progress made in the Benson and Hedges Cup had been but the prelude to far greater deeds in the other one-day competitions. After an unimpressive start to the Sunday League programme with two defeats from the first five fixtures, three successive victories had taken Somerset joint-top of the table by the time attention turned to the Gillette Cup. How could they then have known that by the first weekend of September, they would be battling for both titles?

Warwickshire were the Gillette first round opponents at Taunton and the locals hooted with laughter as openers Amiss and Smith emerged ghost-like in utterly anonymous white crash helmets. Their batting, however, soon won respect and the runs rattled along so smoothly that when Amiss was third out at 128 for a finely-struck 70 the scoring rate was already up to four per over. This proved only the platform for a sustained assault by the captain, Whitehouse, and Humpage who hammered out 150 runs in only 27 overs. Whitehouse hit 94, Humpage 58 and when Warwickshire exhausted their sixty overs the total was a towering 292 for five.

Somerset's task looked hopeless for, to win, they would have

The memorable Somerset squad of 1978. Back row (left to right): Jennings, Moseley, Roebuck, Garner, Dredge, Ian, Marks, and Slocombe. Front row: Russom, Burgess, Denning, Rose, Taylor, Richards and Breakwell.

to score the highest total by a side batting second – ironically the record had been set by Warwickshire in 1976 – and when Rose was out with 17 scored, players and public alike were resigned to defeat.

All had reckoned without the amazing Viv Richards. He saw off a searching examination by Bob Willis, played with a caution few had ever seen and, with Peter Denning an ideal partner, steadily stepped up the scoring rate so well that when tea was taken after 25 overs, Somerset, at 116 for one, were already four ahead of Warwickshire at the same stage.

A miracle was now being tentatively talked of, so dedicated and responsible had Richards become, but a possibly crucial moment came soon after the resumption. Willis came back and at last bowled Denning for 60 to end a county record stand for limited-overs games of 137, scored in 25 overs.

In gathering gloom – the batsmen rejected an invitation to come off for bad light – Willis walked almost back to the

Below left: Batting against Glamorgan early in the season: a match in the Schweppes championships.

boundary, wound himself up, bounded in and bowled his fastest over of the summer. Twice he appealed loudly for a catch behind, twice he was turned down and off his last ball Richards swung him furiously and triumphantly to the legside boundary. In that moment the match was won and lost. Roebuck (45) helped him add 96 in 17 overs; only Botham flopped, to the fans' indignation, needlessly hooking into a fielder's hands. Finally Richards lofted straight for six clean over the pavilion to take Somerset to an astonishing 297 for four with some seventeen balls to spare. He had made 139 not out.

'We just didn't believe we could be beaten,' admitted Warwickshire's bemused Whitehouse. There was no question of Somerset being beaten in the second round against Glamorgan at Cardiff after 'Dasher' Denning, dropped before he had scored, made 145 – the highest individual limited-overs innings by a Somerset batsman – in a total of 330 for four, which was itself the second highest total in Gillette history. Richards,

Below: The drawn-out, disappointing Benson and Hedges semi-final defeat. Kent's Graham Johnson is the batsman, Lloyd Budd the umpire.

Silver star. The West Country Sportsman of the Year in 1978 (*above*) and (*above right*) deep in study at Weston with Marks, Roebuck, and Slocombe during a John Player League match *v* Warwickshire.

on this occasion, contented himself with a supporting role in a stand of 127, scoring 52 including a quite remarkable sequence of eighteen successive singles. Botham, again out of sorts, scratched fifteen runs. Glamorgan, seeking only medals for gallantry, made 260 and so another record was established, the highest aggregate of runs in a Gillette match.

John Arlott was watching the Glamorgan game and deduced that, although Somerset were a splendid side, if it came to an eventual clash, Kent would always beat them. And it was to Canterbury that Somerset made their pilgrimage in the quarter-finals.

There was more than just a Benson and Hedges Cup semi-final defeat to avenge. Somerset's only previous Gillette Cup final appearance in 1967 had ended in 32-run defeat by Kent; in 1974 – the year of Botham's breakthrough – an exciting semi-final at Canterbury had been lost by three wickets and such was the impression made on the match by the Yeovil youngster that the editor of Wisden was moved to write: 'Botham caught my eye first in a Gillette Cup tie in 1974 at Canterbury; he made only nineteen runs, but in a tight match showed his batting class with his upright style and when fifth choice bowler his persistent attack on the stumps sufficed to remove Cowdrey (Colin) and Shepherd. I would particularly like to see Botham given a (Test) chance while he is young and enthusiastic.'

Torrential rain prevented play on the Wednesday, but surprisingly a start was possible by 11.30 next morning and, even more unexpectedly, Kent, already with the Benson and Hedges Cup under their belt and now hot favourites for the Gillette as well, slid dramatically to 120 all out after winning the toss. The pitch, though slow, was not particularly to blame, although Colin Dredge took four for 23 while the giant 6ft 8in West Indian Joel Garner had the extraordinary figures of 9–6–5–1. Again Botham's part was a supporting role. His one for 33 in nine overs, indeed, was the worst return.

He had his chance, however, when Somerset made a most nervous start to what should have been an easy objective. When Richards and Rose were bowled in successive overs, they had slid to 40 for three. This brought in Botham and the next nine overs brought but six runs. In an atmosphere of acute tension he was badly dropped at mid-off, decided to counter-attack to take off the pressure and lived a perilous life against Underwood, including another glaring dropped catch at deep square leg. He was at the wicket for 80 minutes, made 24 and at last his liberal ration of luck was exhausted when he was bowled at 88 for five.

It left Somerset in the lurch, but the sixth pair Marks and Breakwell, by sensible application, brought the side home in the 47th over. On paper it appeared a comfortable victory; in actuality, it had been a close-run thing.

It scarcely seemed likely that Somerset could be involved in any greater drama during their Cup run, but 16 August and their semi-final against Essex at Taunton was to prove the greatest game played since limited-overs cricket was launched in 1963, far exceeding the drama of Lancashire's moonlit win over Gloucestershire in 1971. This was to be the Warwickshire game all over again, but in reverse and with lashings more icing on the cake.

Somerset, winning the toss and losing Slocombe to the seventh ball of the match, were then propelled to a position of apparent impregnability by the great Richards with a quite unstoppable 116. They totalled 287 for six and the most spectacular shot, in the words of admiring skipper Rose, was when 'Richards stepped outside his leg stump and smashed the left-arm spinner Ray East high over extra cover for six. Who else in a semi-final would have had the confidence and ability to play that shot?' Not Ian Botham, who tried to do just that when he had scored a mere seven and was embarrassingly bowled.

Essex went out to bat exactly in the same frame of mind that had assailed Somerset when they attempted their token reply to Warwickshire way back in the first round, and the similarity was stressed as they quickly lost a wicket. Now, however, with Graham Gooch in fine form, they too arrived ahead of target at 119 for two after 25 overs. As the total continued to mount Rose desperately switched his bowlers, seven were tried, but although a third and fourth wicket went down, the fifth pair Fletcher and Pont appeared to have the match in their pockets as they approached 250 in the 55th over.

And now, at last, Botham brought his brilliance to bear on Somerset's cause. Pont tried for a two to deep cover point, Botham ran round, flung back all in one movement and the batsman was run out. Next over Fletcher off-drove forcefully at Botham and in a flash the bowler had held onto the stinging return catch. When Phillip, backing up, slipped, fell and was run out in the same over, while Botham came back to bowl Turner in his next over, it seemed as though Essex, at 266 for eight, were dead.

Six runs from the 59th over, however, took them to 276 for eight. Twelve wanted, six balls left and the bowler Dredge went slowly back to his mark like a condemned criminal. A single, an edged four and then East was bowled, but Dredge's fourth ball was a no ball – worse, Somerset's sharpest fielder, Slocombe, overthrew the wicket in his anxiety and three runs were snatched. Nothing came from the next delivery, one from the sixth and so to the last ball. Three wanted, Lever the batsman, every fielder back on the boundary, a furious heave, frantic split

Joy unconfined. Ian and Colin Dredge mobbed after the amazing Gillette semi-final against Essex.

seconds as everyone tried to sight where the ball had gone, Lever and Smith sprinting one, two, turning for the third and Rose, careering into extra cover space, picking up, hurling in and wicketkeeper Taylor gathering and launching himself headlong at the stumps in the same movement.

The scores were level, but Somerset were through to the Cup final and a clash with Sussex because they had lost fewer wickets. 'I have never seen a more thrilling cricket match,' enthused adjudicator Jim Laker. No more needed saying.

So Somerset had made it to Lord's. But more, much more than that, they had set themselves up for the most challenging weekend any county had encountered.

For, concurrent with their spectacular progress to the Gillette Cup final, they had reeled off nine Sunday victories interrupted only by one washed-out match, which had left them clear at the top of the John Player League table. Victory would be vital in the final game against Essex for their nearest challengers Hampshire had a superior run rate and would pip them on the post if Somerset were to lose.

So here was a situation in which a county which had never won anything in its 103-year history had the chance of clinching the Gillette Cup on Saturday, 2 September, before travelling back to Taunton for their final Sunday game the following

113

afternoon, victory in which would guarantee the John Player League title, too.

There was one snag. They were committed to the Fenner Trophy festival at Scarborough from Wednesday to Friday – a four-county knock-out tournament, the final of which was being played the day before the Gillette. So Somerset faced the possibility of a 300-mile trip to London the night before the Lord's showpiece. Their opening game was on the Wednesday and, said a member of the side: 'We'll simply lose it.' That was precisely what happened and if it was unfortunate for the festival organisers it was the only course any county would have taken.

It had rained for much of the week so it was a happy surprise to find sunshine bathing Lord's on Saturday morning. The trains had been piling into Paddington from an early hour, carrying some of the lucky 4,000 ticket-holders. Others, like Botham's father, had been driving since before dawn. The allocation of tickets had been a bad business. Somerset and Sussex had each received only 4,000, less even than their membership figures and, to protests, Lord's had lamely suggested they should have spoken up at the previous winter's Test and County Cricket Board annual meeting and urged a larger allocation. That reasoning was really fairly fatuous because the smaller fry like Somerset would have had little chance of influencing the 'establishment' counties, some of whom might have found difficulty in selling 4,000 tickets had they been there at the final.

Lord's, however, was filled as it always is for a Gillette final, although the credentials of many in the crowd would not have borne too searching a scrutiny. Few could have forecast the appearance of Sussex in the final. They had been ripped apart by the mid-season departure of the disgraced Tony Greig. Arnold Long, resuscitated after many years at Surrey, had done a marvellous job in shaping a new-look Sussex (or rather, an old-look Surrey, since several of the side had seen better days at The Oval). Their progress to the final had hardly inspired optimism, either.

A first round six-wicket win over Suffolk had been followed by a hair-raising two-run margin over Staffordshire and a nine-run defeat of Yorkshire which was devalued by the 10-overs-a-side nature of the match. Only in beating Lancashire by 136 runs in the semi-finals had they shown real ability, and had they not been soundly beaten by Somerset in the Benson and Hedges Cup earlier in the summer? It was no wonder that the bookies made Somerset odds-on favourites and refused further bets on a week-end double of Gillette and John Player.

Zummerzet! The fans transform sedate Lord's on Gillette Cup final day.

Ray Illingworth, the old England captain, summed it up on Saturday morning by saying: 'The pressure of being so close to their first honour will be a severe test for Somerset. But it is one I believe they will pass with flying colours.'

This air of optimism was infectious for when, on being invited to bat by a blatantly defensive Long, Rose punched three fours and fourteen runs off Imran Khan's opening wayward over, Somerset fans simply sat back, punctured the first barrels of scrumpy and prepared for another run feast from their favourites. With Richards to come how could they be wrong?

But things did go wrong, badly wrong. Richards, weighed down with responsibility after a pre-match Press build-up that only stopped short at suggesting the second coming of Christ,

was reluctant to play his shots, and the scoring rate slowed to a trickle as the spinners Cheatle and Barclay and the accurate medium-paced Spencer began to exert a stranglehold. Worse, wickets went down. Denning had gone for a duck; Rose, after batting fluently for 30, was caught behind off Cheatle; the same bowler committed Roebuck on the front foot with a slow ball, a full toss, and induced a ballooned catch to mid-on.

With three wickets down for 73 and 24 overs gone, out came Botham, grimly aware of his debt to Somerset. His skipper Rose had said only earlier in the week: 'Ian owes us some runs this season, but I've got a feeling that this weekend he is going to come good for us.'

Only 20 runs had been scored in the previous eleven overs and Botham, as so often, immediately took his life in his hands and started hitting out. Once, twice he hoisted Cheatle gloriously over the square leg boundary for six. With Richards still in occupation, hopes of a high score again soared, but the West Indian was ill at ease, swatting unsuccessfully at the tantalising Cheatle. When he reached the other end he tried to emulate Botham, but his hook was underweighted and fell straight into Arnold's hands at deep square leg. Sussex fielders sprinted to deluge Arnold in backslaps and Richards departed, cursing, for a 44 that had never fired the imagination.

So Botham now stood on the burning deck, straining to force shots as Marks holed out in frustration at his failure to time the ball and Burgess set off on a fool's errand and had no hope of twisting his heavyweight frame into a U-turn to regain his ground. This brought Taylor to join him at 157 in the 48th over and the wicketkeeper seemed to be wearing weighted boots. With only twenty runs in the previous ten overs even singles were now something of a celebration, but Taylor made matters worse by an exasperating penchant for pinching the bowling off the last ball of each over.

As the overs seeped away, Botham started throwing his bat at every ball in a vainglorious bid to give his side a challenging score. One shot off the speedy old Test bowler Arnold was quite breathtaking. From outside off stump he threw every ounce of his considerable strength into the hook shot and sent the ball into the lower tier of the square leg stand. Going for the same shot in the 59th over from Imran Khan he perished superbly, clean bowled for a quite brilliant 80 made out of 121. The long-standing debt to Somerset had been repaid.

The power hitting of Joel Garner in the few remaining balls just showed what an error Rose had made in not promoting the West Indian above Taylor in the batting order. Taylor had taken the last twelve overs to scrape thirteen runs at a time

Somerset should have been sprinting. Even so, a score of 207 for seven was the first Gillette final total over 200 in five years.

Sussex, though, needed to score at only three and a half runs per over and the two opening maidens meant nothing, although Mendis survived a catch to square leg in the second of these. Mendis and Barclay were not rated among the best of county openers, but they saw off the menace of Botham and Garner, not without some painful knocks, and kept up a rapid scoring rate. They were nearly halfway to their target and almost up to four an over when Mendis at last mis-hit to be caught at 93 in the 24th over.

Now came an amazing turn of events immediately after tea. Botham and Garner came back and both struck at 106. Barclay went to hook Botham, mistimed and was caught at wide mid-on; next, Javed Miandad, the first of two potential Pakistani match-winners, was brilliantly taken right-handed by Taylor. In the next over, the 29th, Botham, as near to a snorting bull as a bowler can be, dug in a bouncer at the dangerous Imran Khan, who ducked desperately, lost his cap and bore at least the brunt of the delivery on his head. Botham paced back, pounded in again and sent down another short-lifter. Imran had anticipated the ball and, in cringing crouch, stuck out his bat in surrender and lobbed up the easiest caught and bowled. Botham was buried beneath his colleagues as he took the catch. An impregnable tea-time 97 for one had turned into a tottering 110 for four and the suspectedly fragile Sussex were teetering on the brink of a complete nervous breakdown.

One more wicket and Somerset would surely have been through them to a long tail. Rose, however, could not risk bowling out Botham and Garner, in case of a close finish. The two Pauls, Parker and Phillipson, survived one more assault from the pace pair and then Rose was obliged to turn to the friendlier medium pace of Burgess and Jennings while bitterly regretting the injury to Breakwell that had put Somerset in the field without a spinner to provide variety to their attack.

With plentiful overs to play with, Parker and Phillipson could afford to pick their runs, and gradually the Sussex crisis passed until it was plain sailing to success. Rose brought back Botham for one final assault but, with understandable desperation in a depressing situation, he bowled badly and short and only speeded up the end. Phillipson was not to see it, being caught with the scores level, but Parker suitably clipped the four that took Sussex home in the 54th over with five wickets in hand. Parker, 62 not out, was Ken Barrington's Man of the Match. Poor Somerset could only complain that this award, at least, could have gone to Botham as a consolation.

Gillette Cup Final Lords

Somerset

Rose	c Long	b Cheatle	30
Denning		b Imran Khan	0
Richards	c Arnold	b Barclay	44
Roebuck	c Mendis	b Cheatle	9
Botham		b Imran Khan	80
Marks	c Arnold	b Barclay	4
Burgess		run out	3
Taylor		not out	13
Garner		not out	8
Jennings			
Extras (lb 10, nb 6)			16
Total		(7 wickets – 60 overs)	207

Fall of wickets: 1–22, 2–53, 3–73, 4–115, 5–151, 6–157, 7–194
Bowling: Imran Khan 12–1–50–2, Arnold 12–2–43–0,
Spencer 12–3–27–0, Cheatle 12–3–50–2, Barclay 12–3–21–2

Sussex

Umpires
H. D. Bird
B. J. Meyer

Man of the match
Paul Parker

Barclay	c Roebuck	b Botham	44
Mendis	c Marks	b Burgess	44
Parker		not out	62
Javed Miandad	c Taylor	b Garner	0
Imran Khan		c and b Botham	3
Phillipson	c Taylor	b Dredge	32
Storey		not out	0
Long			
Spencer			
Arnold			
Cheatle			
Extras (b 1, lb 9, w 7, nb 9)			26
Total		(5 wickets – 53·1 overs)	211

Fall of wickets: 1–93, 2–106, 3–106, 4–110, 5–207
Bowling: Garner 12–3–34–1, Dredge 10–2–26–1,
Botham 12–1–65–2, Jennings 9–1–29–0, Burgess 10–2–27–1,
Denning 0·1–0–4–0

Sussex won by 5 wickets

Failure, but a fond farewell to their fans. Rose, Ian, Denning, and Marks leave the Lord's balcony after the final with a last salute to their marvellous fans.

It had been Rose's abiding fear, as his side faced their momentous weekend double assault, that Gillette defeat could destroy them. 'We aim to get the Gillette Cup out of the way first. If we win that we can go out on Sunday and enjoy ourselves,' he said. 'If we don't then we will be under double the pressure.'

No cider celebrations had been the instruction for Saturday night, win or lose, but nobody felt like it, anyway. Botham was driven back to Somerset in almost total silence.

BBC television crews were at both Bournemouth and Taunton for the Sunday showdown. Although Somerset held a four-point lead at the top of the table, Hampshire, with a superior overall run rate, could still overhaul them if they beat Middlesex in their final game, while Somerset were beaten by Essex.

	P	W	L	No Rst	Pts
Somerset	15	11	2	2	48
Hampshire	15	10	3	2	44

The odds against beating Essex had lengthened alarmingly. Saturday had been such a certainty – 7–4 on – and defeat had come as a severe shock. Now they were in the corner and no Somerset bookie, chairman Len Creed included, was too happy about taking money on an Essex win.

Sunday, 3 September, like the previous day, dawned superbly fine. The Indian summer, after such appalling weather in the previous three months, had arrived. Most supporters had hurried home from London for the match, but there were plenty of Somerset stragglers on the 9.30 am out of Paddington. The mood was still strictly optimistic for all the nagging doubts among the club committee. No county had faced such a challenging weekend, and if the Gillette had been lost to bad nerves, bad decisions, bad form but, perhaps most of all, to wiser if older heads on Sussex shoulders, it seemed inconceivable that Sunday was going to double the disappointment.

Several shops in Taunton had posters proclaiming the invincibility of their team; at midday, two hours before the game would begin, the ground was already almost full, although the gates would remain open to accommodate standing room only about which no one would complain. The sun by noon was scorching, the Ring of Bells was doing a roaring trade in takeaway orders, and in the dingy dressing room Rose was doing his best to raise spirits.

Essex and their captain Keith Fletcher, however, had not travelled to Taunton to be the guests at an orgy of Somerset self-congratulation. Of all the counties he could have been playing in this final fixture, Rose would have opted last for Essex. The memory of that amazing Gillette semi-final only eighteen days earlier was unnerving enough, but even more was now at stake. Like Somerset, Essex had won nothing in their 101-year existence. To save themselves the embarrassment of being left the only bridesmaids in county cricket, they had to stop Somerset today. The stakes, then, were high as Rose and Fletcher walked out to the wicket to toss up.

First round to Rose. He won, put Essex in and led his fielders out to a colossal roar from a carnival crowd. The optimism seemed in order, too, as tight bowling by Botham and Moseley, who had returned to replace Garner, not contracted for Sunday games, and greyhound sprinting by Slocombe, Richards and others put Essex in awful trouble at 29 for three. But there the celebrating had to stop for once again Fletcher and Pont, who had so petrified Somerset in the Gillette semi-final, staged a 63-run revival.

That proved but the prelude to a crucial last eleven overs in which the now free-flowing Fletcher, in alliance with an unrecognisably aggressive Brian Hardie, savaged Somerset for 98 runs. Fletcher finished unbeaten on 76, Hardie was not out until the last ball, Essex totalled 190 for five from their forty overs and Somerset faced a fierce challenge.

Almost immediately they were in trouble with both openers falling while the score stuck on 18 – poor Rose, in the midst of permanent nightmare, returning to the pavilion with his face a

sheer shroud of misery. Richards and Roebuck tried hard to repair the innings, but in their efforts to improve the scoring rate both perished and Somerset's predicament was 87 for four.

Botham by now was at the wicket, his cause no less acute than twenty-four hours earlier, but there was both booming self-confidence and considerable faith in that guardian angel hovering again over his shoulder. He had in support the stylish young Slocombe who, in hindsight, many felt should have been in for Marks the previous day as well.

Botham took up from where he had left off at Lord's, and soon the canny Fletcher had his fielders in full retreat and wringing their hands when unwise enough to try cutting off some bludgeoning square and cover drives.

Essex Taunton September 3

Essex

Lilley	c Denning	b Burgess	13
Gooch	c Burgess	b Botham	7
McEwan		b Moseley	2
Fletcher		not out	76
Pont		b Dredge	35
Hardie		b Botham	38
Phillip			
Turner			
East			
Smith			
Lever			
Extras (lb 16, nb 3)			19
Total		(5 wickets – 40 overs)	190

Fall of wickets: 1–16, 2–25, 3–29, 4–92, 5–190
Bowling: Botham 8–0–38–2, Moseley 8–0–20–1, Burgess 8–0–20–1, Jennings 8–0–38–0, Dredge 8–0–55–1

Somerset

Umpires
W. E. Alley
D. J. Halfyard

Rose		b Lever	9
Denning	c Smith	b Phillip	8
Richards	c Hardie	b Gooch	26
Roebuck		b East	30
Botham	c McEwan	b Phillip	45
Slocombe		b Lever	20
Burgess		c and b Turner	0
Jennings		not out	14
Dredge		b Lever	14
Taylor		run out	4
Moseley		run out	0
Extras (b 2, lb 12, nb 3)			18
Total		(40 overs)	188

Fall of wickets: 1–18, 2–18, 3–69, 4–87, 5–137, 6–140, 7–157, 8–177, 9–185
Bowling: Lever 8–0–38–3, Phillip 8–0–35–2, Gooch 8–0–31–1, Turner 8–0–32–1, East 8–0–34–1

Essex won by 2 runs

Now this magnificent young athlete, who had so handsomely repaid his debt to Somerset the previous day, was giving double value in the way which had made him a national hero. He was living utterly outrageously, offering three extremely difficult chances and one, when he had made 31, which was badly put down at long-on. Slocombe he had lost at 137 after their fighting stand of 50 had provided the perfect instance of youth having its fling.

The news, by now, had come that Hampshire had comfortably beaten Middlesex at Bournemouth. Gordon Greenidge, with a glorious 122, had propelled them to 221 for four, Middlesex had managed only 195 in reply and the Bournemouth crowd was now clustered around a wide screen watching Somerset's frantic fight for runs.

Fifty-eight had been needed with ten overs to go, but even Botham does not enjoy inexhaustible luck and at last he holed out in the grand manner, hooked defiantly to deep square leg to be seventh out at 157 for an invaluable 45.

In these desperate circumstances Dredge and Jennings kept running at every opportunity and as yet another heart-stopping finish unfolded in this treasured Taunton season so unflappable Essex began to make mistakes amid overthrows and scampered leg byes.

Dredge was bowled, but Taylor, transformed from the stooge of Lord's, began swiping away so that the last over arrived in incredibly similar circumstances to that Gillette semi-final. Then Essex, at 276 for eight, had needed twelve to win; now Somerset, at 179 for eight, needed eleven to tie, for, such was the Sunday League ruling, that the two points awarded for such a result would be enough to ensure finishing above Hampshire.

Taylor and Jennings scrambled six runs from the first four balls of Phillip's final over, but in trying to turn a single into a two Taylor was run out. Last man Moseley came in, swung and missed but made the leg bye.

So came the climax. Jennings faced the final ball needing four runs for the tie. Like Lever eighteen days earlier, he swung desperately, the ball swept out to long leg, they ran two and kept running as wicketkeeper Smith, having rushed to meet long leg's return, dashed back to break the wicket. He could have tripped, had hiccoughs, been struck by a meteorite. There was no such divine intervention and Moseley was run out.

Somerset's dressing room was awash and it was not with cider. As the disaster of their double weekend defeat sunk home, for Ian Botham it was a bitter lesson that when you seem to bestride the world, the game of cricket can kick you down in an instant and leave you with only shattered dreams.

Close Encounters

It was one of those exhilarating Gillette Cup days at Taunton with 10,000 crammed into the ground and Somerset sweating and not only in the sunshine. Quarter-final opponents Surrey, fresh from unexpectedly winning the Benson and Hedges Cup, were looking to continue their Cup success and at 108 for one in the thirty-fourth over were well on course for a winning total.

Ian Botham, still flushed from his heroic deeds against Hampshire only four weeks earlier, was bowling and Geoff Howarth played him forcefully down to deep third man where the deceptively waddling Merv Kitchen was on patrol. Howarth and John Edrich scampered a single, but the New Zealander then turned for the two and was almost in hand-shaking reach of his captain wher Edrich firmly ruled 'No' which sent Howarth chasing back.

Meanwhile Kitchen had gathered and hurled back to the bowler's end, but Botham, fearing the ball would not reach him in time, advanced some seven yards down the wicket to collect Kitchen's throw, then whipped round and shied down the stumps. Howarth was well out and a roar of delight echoed around the ground.

But the drama was not over. As Howarth walked out, the Skipper strode purposefully towards Botham. It is an unnerving experience to see that indestructible dome bearing down on you when the brows are more beetled than ever, the eyes laser-like in their intent, the mouth tight-lipped, the jaw set like cement. One should quaver before such a Brian Close, especially when he bawls out: 'You daft bugger . . . you took a bloody risk shying at the stumps when you had time to run back with the ball and break the wicket.'

'The bloody sticks are flattened, aren't they?' shouted back the 18-year-old Botham.

Such cordiality between Close and his bucking young colt was to become a feature of Ian's formative years with Somerset.

At the Oval on another Gillette occasion when Botham, back on the long-off boundary, had no hope of reaching a skied catch,

Close shouted across that vast arena: 'Wake up, Ian' to be answered by an arm flung in furious helplessness.

After such an outburst between them, Close would be relaxing in the dressing room or having a drink at the end of the day. 'Suddenly,' recalls Close, 'I'd be aware of this big, strapping lad standing beside me sheepishly and saying "I'm sorry about what I said to you today, skipper, I didn't really mean it."

'And, of course, I bore him no grudge. What happens on the field is in the heat of the moment and you've forgotten about it by the end of the day.

'The thing about Ian is that he is so tremendously enthusiastic that his blood can boil over in the tension of a game. I understood his angry reaction that day he shied at the wicket and I bawled him out, but there was a lesson to be learned and it was my job to teach him.'

That Close was captain of Somerset as Ian came into the side was undoubtedly crucial in his development to what he is today. For all his burning ambition and enthusiasm, Ian was wild and needed a strong skipper. No Regimental Sergeant Major could have done a better job than Brian Close.

Somerset were, indeed, inspired in inviting Close to join them after his bitter abandonment by Yorkshire at the end of 1970. He thought, however, he was going down West to graze and suddenly found himself shepherding a flock of frisky lambs. A retirement that might have come around the time Ian made the team was put off until weakening illnesses and weary legs told him it was time to go in 1977.

'Somerset gave me a new, or extended, lease of life, but it was tough,' concedes Close. 'Here I was with this marvellous team of young talent and I had to keep them on their toes. I never used to take any food during a day's play – just a pot of tea to keep me going – otherwise I would have dozed off and what sort of example would that have been?'

The way in which Close coaxed, cajoled and cursed his kids – in their own cricketing interests – led to a popular misconception of another row with Botham. Midway through the 1975 season rumours of a rebellion against Close started filtering through to Fleet Street. Piece by piece, from quiet words here and innuendo there, was produced a splash story that Close was being too tough on the kids and they had complained to the committee. By implication, and because he was the most prominent player among them, Botham was inferred to be at the back of it, although this was never actually printed.

Close tells a completely different story, of moans from the more senior members of the team. 'If a youngster was upset then

the reason was that I had realised our only title hope for the season rested in the Sunday League, and that meant making sure our Sunday team kept their eye in during the midweek matches which, in turn, meant that a lad who wasn't suited to Sunday cricket had to be left out of the team.'

Botham, anyway, could never have been party to a Close conspiracy. For all the rowing ȏn the field, they were firm friends and he had too much respect for his skipper. As recently as the eve of England's setting out for Australia for the 1978–79 Ashes tour, Ian and Kathryn had arranged to drive over to Close's house at Baildon in Yorkshire for the express purpose of picking Brian's brain about the pitfalls of playing on an Australian tour. The pub door accident in Doncaster the previous night prevented the meeting.

Something of a father-son affiliation seems to have existed between two rather kindred characters right from the start.

'I knew nothing about Ian when one day towards the end of the 1973 season we were short of players through injuries and the committee said "Look, we've got this ground staff lad up at Lord's. Why not give him a game?"' recalls Close.

'He was keen, enthusiastic, full of confidence. We had to watch him, tell him what to do. Cricket's a thinking game and youngsters don't think.

'Ian was desperately keen to learn. Many times I'd drive him home from a match – unusual for me and yes, he doesn't like to hang about behind a steering wheel, either – and I'd spend the journey talking to him about mistakes he might have made and how to put them right.'

Their friendship went further than that. 'My wife Vivienne and I had these good friends Gerry and Jan Waller who lived not far from us at Thorne in Yorkshire. They used to come to the Yorkshire games and when I went to Somerset they would come and watch them, too. They had two daughters who'd come and that's how Kathryn came to meet Ian. Now, of course, they're married and producing a family – Yorkshire-born! – and she's a grand girl for Ian. She's the level-headed one who prefers to stay out of Ian's limelight, but she has a good steadying influence on him.'

And he still needs it, too. Close says: 'He's like a five-furlong sprinter, trying to do everything at once.

'When he bowls he tries something different with every ball and when it goes wrong and he gets hit he loses his rag and bowls rubbish as he did towards the end of that Gillette Cup final. All he has to remember is length and direction, but not Ian – he tries to do the lot. When you try and do a lot of things your margin for error is that much larger.

'And when he bats and hits a four he wants to do it again next ball regardless of its merits. He's got all the shots in the book, but he's got to discipline himself and pick the balls to hit.'

If Close seems somewhat harsh on Ian's shortcomings, when there have been so many marvellous performances packed into so short a career, then that is nothing to the day Ian followed his 108 against Pakistan at Lord's with the eight for 34 that wrapped up the match before lunch on the Monday. Close, now only committed to Todmorden cricket, had joined the BBC TV Test team as the resident expert analyst.

Botham was already in the bar feeling pretty well pleased with his work when Close came in. Says Ian: 'I had hardly got a pint in my hand before Brian was giving me a terrific rollicking for flashing my bat too much at balls outside the off-stump. Obviously I'm not going to get a big head while he's around!'

Close comments: 'I did say "congratulations" first before blasting him. I always do.'

There is a case, of course, for saying that, taking his great talent into consideration, Ian Botham's rapid rise to world-class owes a little to the intrusion on international cricket of one Kerry Packer.

Most of the overseas stars, the Australians excepted, playing *now* for Packer came over to England each summer to play for their adopted counties and have done for some years. Their effect has been to 'level out' the respective strengths of counties and has led to some great successes by sides one would have classed as Cinderellas in the past. Worcestershire, Hampshire, Leicestershire, Northamptonshire and, latterly, Somerset and Essex are obvious examples. That has made county cricket the more competitive and can only be a good thing for the game.

It also had the converse effect of immensely strengthening touring countries who would, in the past, have provided easy opposition for England in the intervening years between the Ashes battles.

The reason this happened is that there is no finer scholarship in the learning of cricket than on the playing fields of England. Only here are cricketers liable to face a different set of circumstances every day – wet wickets, sticky wickets, hard wickets, swing, spin, conventional three-day cricket, one-day Cup-ties, 40-over Sunday slogs.

These overseas stars became so finely attuned to English conditions that a Test at Lord's was no different to them than a day in Karachi or Kingston, Jamaica. They could cope with the effects of whichever climate they encountered.

If Kerry Packer had not then creamed off all but a few, it is an argument for debate whether England would win so many matches as they do these days. As it is, England are likely to remain on top in Test cricket until such time as either a non-Packer-tainted crop of new overseas cricketers come and learn with English counties, or World Series Cricket comes to some sort of compromise with the authorities and the Packer stars are again allowed to play for their countries in official Test cricket.

At the moment the new crop of overseas Test batsmen have been unable to cope with Botham's swing bowling. They have not played off the back foot and have had neither feet nor head near the ball.

The Skipper in typical shot. Warwickshire's Deryck Murray keeps wicket. The ball, inevitably, has been hoisted high.

Brian Close will not be drawn on the quality of the countries England has played since Botham's explosive arrival in the team, but he does recall the 'wetting of the baby's head' when Ian was picked for two Prudential Trophy one-day games against the all-conquering West Indians of 1976 and did not do too well. 'He looked a bit out of his depth, didn't he?'

Close, nonetheless, can also recall quite breathtaking batting by Ian against that self-same West Indian touring team of 1976, when he hit 56 for Somerset at Taunton, and again for his county in their historic victory over the Australians in 1977 at Bath before the tourists' concentration was rocked by the disclosure of the Kerry Packer coup.

It is mean – and meaningless – therefore to detract from Ian's outstanding achievements. He has taken the wickets and hit the hundreds and that is what matters.

If Packer, meanwhile, will not go away, then the likelihood of Ian being tempted in the near future by mercenary money is rather more than remote. He is immensely proud of being part of Mike Brearley's England team and his lifestyle is very comfortable within the now well-paid-at-the-top Establishment game.

He is well liked by his England colleagues who probably know him even better than the Somerset lads, he has a ready smile, a good sense of humour and always signs for the autograph hunters. Success has not spoilt him.

Brian Close considers, however, that he must try to control his high-spirited aggression on the field. DB was not amused to see Botham bearing down the wicket, full into the face of the television cameras, aiming a contemptuous finger at a dismissed Australian batsman in the 1978-79 Ashes series, a finger that some mistakenly construed as a V-sign although the sentiment was still the same. He says, anyway, that Ian believes that the baiting of batsmen with a few well-chosen words from his position in the slips is all part of the game.

Under the captaincy of Close and in a successful England side, the best has been brought out of Botham. Will it continue to happen with Somerset, a side striving still for their first title after any number of narrow misses? Once the breakthrough comes, they could well dominate county cricket in the next few years. Much will depend upon Close's successor, Brian Rose, one of whose principal tasks will be the way he handles his volcanic virtuoso Botham. Rose is a quiet young man, serious and deep-thinking and there are those who think a harder, more experienced player might have been chosen for the considerable task of succeeding Close, particularly in benefitting from Botham's full potential. Rose, though, has started well.

As Close says: 'Ian is full of good things, but he is impulsive and hot-blooded and he needs someone standing over him.

'In truth, he is only a boy who, in many respects, is still growing up.'

The growing-up boy, however, has a lot going for him. Says Close: 'I'll state this – Ian is going to become one of the greatest of English batsmen when he has learnt to discipline himself. He comes in halfway down the order at present because he is regarded as an all-rounder and that is where they go in, but this boy's biggest quality is his batting and nobody's yet realised it.

'People are praising David Gower and he's a grand little stroke player, but Ian's potential is so much better. He is a marvellous stroke player, who hits the ball as hard as anyone I can think of. When he matures and isn't trying to do everything all the time this is for what he will become famous.'

But what about the guardian angel who sits so securely on Ian's shoulder? 'Yes, he has had his share of luck. What successful person in life hasn't? But Ian Botham has got a damned sight more ability than most of his England colleagues.'

Oh, yes, there is something else to say about our young hero. It's 'Both' as in 'moth'. Not 'Boath' as in 'loath', as television and radio commentators would have us believe. None of his cricketing contemporaries use the media's misinformed pronunciation. Mum may think that their interpretation makes the name sound somewhat more refined; Leslie Botham is a 'Both' as in 'moth' man. Of the brilliant Botham there is one more side the public does not see, unless there is a clue in his stumbling attempts to answer questions at television interviews. 'Ian,' says Close, 'is reasonably rational about his success. For all his acclaim, he has a certain humility.'

Gorilla Warfare

It barely seemed credible that the young man who left the departure lounge of Heathrow's Terminal 3 on 24 October 1978 in answer to the call for the 21.45 Flight QF 002 to Australia was a sportsman, still less that he would have a principal part to play in England's fight to retain the Ashes against their oldest cricketing enemies. His brand-new blazer was slung around his shoulders, his left arm was heavily bandaged inside a sling.

Forty-eight hours earlier Ian Botham had thrust his hand out to open a pub door after farewell drinks in Doncaster and plunged through the plate glass, badly gashing the tendons of his left wrist. He was rushed to hospital to have maybe ten stitches inserted. The cuts would heal, he was told, but he could forget about playing cricket for several weeks. It was not until next morning that the doctors would discharge him from Doncaster Royal Infirmary.

An ashen Ian explained: 'It was a sheer accident. Luckily it was not my bowling hand.'

Indestructability, of course, could be Botham's middle name. England's travelling physiotherapist, Bernard Thomas, was unperturbed. 'Ian's a tough lad,' he said, 'and I am confident he will be in the team for the first Test.'

My own newspaper, the *Daily Mirror*, imprudently questioned this optimism, starting its splash story: 'Ian Botham . . . is doubtful for the first Test on December 1.'

Ian was incensed at what he saw as a slur on his strength and resilience and had plenty of hot words for the first *Mirror* man he met. Maybe, however, it helped to harden his resolve to meet that 1 December deadline. But, if the previous winter in Pakistan had been a frustration, that was nothing to his exasperation at enforced idleness during his first fortnight in Australia. He had so much he wanted to prove to the Australian public after his miserable Whitbread-sponsored winter in Melbourne two years earlier when it had been made plain to him that players and public did not think much of his ability. Now he had to sit around while colleagues got into Test trim.

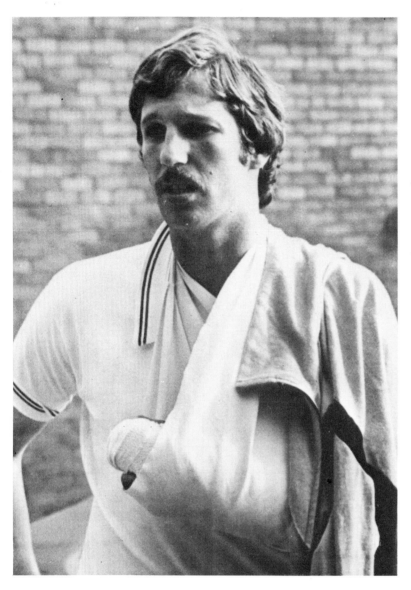

Yet only twenty-six days after the Doncaster accident he was pronounced fit to play against New South Wales in Sydney – a full fortnight ahead of the first Test. His rapid recovery was quite remarkable and a relief to the England party, whose tour had started on a low note with a 32-run defeat by South Australia in Adelaide and a tame draw with Victoria in Melbourne.

He underlined his astonishing powers of recovery when, with only a few net practices behind him, he strode out to hit a typically aggressive 56 and, after New South Wales had been forced to follow on without any wickets for Botham, he then

Previous spread: Walking on air! The way the Aussie batsmen saw Ian. This is the fourth Test, at Sydney.

Above left: Now look what a fine mess I've got into! Leaving hospital after the Doncaster accident.

Above: Proud England touring party 1978–79. Taken at Sydney shortly before clinching the Ashes, Ian is fifth left, standing.

scythed through the State side's second innings to finish with five for 51 and ensure a ten-wicket win.

Just why they market tee-shirts in Somerset with the motif 'Bionic Botham' emblazoned across the chest became ever more apparent three nights later when the party had flown on to Brisbane.

His wife Kathryn was with Ian for the start of the tour and they decided on a double dinner celebration. It was the eve of his twenty-third birthday but, much more important, Kathryn was expecting again. In fact, she would be obliged to fly back to England in a few days' time under the regulations on the

137

reluctance of air stewards to adopt the role of aerial angels of midwifery.

What was a happy evening ended in the small hours with Mrs Botham waking up to find her beefy husband rolling around the bed in agony and then vomiting violently. He was suffering from an acute attack of poisoning from his sea food dinner dish.

Any prospect of his playing against Queensland in a few hours' time would have seemed out of the question to anyone other than the unquenchable birthday boy. Ian, of course, snorted at suggestions that he might care to drop out of the side, then faced a day in the field under a burning sun when others would have opted for a few hours' sleep in the dressing room. He finally confounded considered medical opinion by bowling well enough to take three wickets.

His five for 70 in the second innings brought match figures of eight for 133 and a convincing six-wicket win over Queensland. His colleagues expressed no great awe at this superman stuff. For some time now Ian has gloried in the nickname Guy the Gorilla, after a loveable inmate at London Zoo.

Geoff Boycott explained once: 'Ian doesn't know his own strength. When he's on the rampage we get out of the way – he's liable to give you a hug and squeeze you to death! He really has amazing vitality and strength for a young man.'

In the extravagant headlines of the Australian Press they even enlarged on his nickname by labelling him 'The Golden Gorilla' partly because he had become something of a popular villain to an Australian public who appreciated his brash exuberance. They were beginning to boo him good-naturedly and applaud him sincerely. It was nothing new to Ian. In the English season of 1978 it had happened on several grounds and only in front of that most myopic of cricket crowds – Canterbury – was the barracking of Botham genuinely hostile.

When the battle for the Ashes opened in Brisbane later in the week Botham made an immediate impact. Australia, on winning the toss, were caught in heavy conditions and crashed incredibly to 26 for six, then 53 for seven before the eighth pair Maclean and Hogg added 60 to help their side to an all out 116, Botham bagging three for 40.

Derek Randall, borne to Australia on the reputation of his 174 in the Centenary Test of 1977 in Melbourne, was top scorer with 75 in England's total of 286, but the liveliest batting of the innings came from the two youngsters, Botham and Gower. They put on 95 for the sixth wicket, Gower getting 44 and Botham falling one short of his 50.

Australia's new captain Graham Yallop (102) and Kim Hughes (129) then suggested there was nothing really wrong

Meanwhile, back home at Doncaster . . . Kathryn displays the latest pride of the Botham family, Sarah.

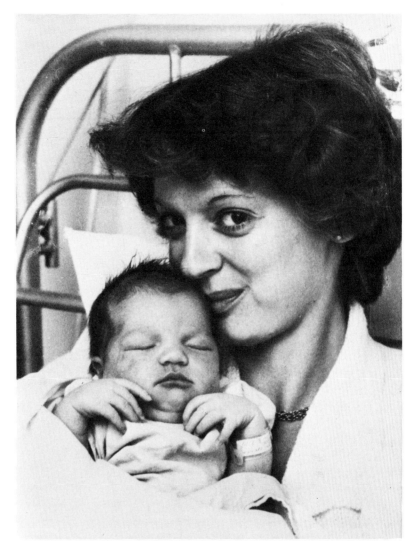

with the new post-Packer Australian era by putting on 170 together and swelling Australia's second innings to 339. England, set 170, got home by seven wickets with Randall again excelling with an unbeaten 74, but it had been a well-fought Test with little to suggest the agony ahead for the Aussies.

Next port of call was Perth and on an unexpectedly awkward pitch, Botham had a ball. He took four for 16 and followed it with four for 37 as Western Australia, scourge of recent touring teams, were wiped out for 52 and 78 to leave England with a 140-run win.

The second Test took place on the same ground four days later and any fears about the state of the wicket were soon dispelled despite a dreadful start – 3 for two – as Boycott (77)

Ashes enemies. Hogg (*left*) ducks a Botham bouncer, while (*above*) Botham gets the better of Hogg with the bat as well. The Aussie took 41 wickets in the series, but only got Ian twice. Notice the different style of the head guards.

and Gower (102) put on 158 for the fourth wicket and England went on to 309.

Australia, 190, only stayed in the match because Peter Toohey battled to an unbeaten 81. Then, although their new fast bowling discovery Rodney Hogg took his second five-wicket haul of the match as England struggled to 208, Australia's target of 328 was too much for them, their last five wickets falling for 20 runs as they were all out for 161.

England, emphatic 166-run winners, were two up in the series and only one victory away from ensuring the retention of the Ashes. The mood was euphoric, yet Ian Botham for once was not his buoyant self. The Perth match had also marked his thirteenth Test and even he proved susceptible to superstition. It was the most uncomplimentary Test of his career. He scored 11 and 30 which was acceptable; it was his bowling that brought him genuine despair. For the first time he failed to take a single wicket, finishing with the unflattering figures of nought for 100.

Fed up with the teasing that followed, he said he would stop drinking and shed some weight. 'I thought I'd bowled well, so it upset me when people began to joke about that nought for 100,' he said. 'I've got to accept that I will get a game like that now and again.' After 70 wickets in 12 Tests, he was due for one.

A few days later Botham was back in more familiar spirits. Christmas had come and, to brighten the depression of being thousands of miles from home, Essex's John Lever dreamed up the idea of all the players wearing a fancy dress costume that started with the letter of the alphabet allotted them at their Christmas party. Ian, of course, was given the letter 'g' and arrived at dinner entirely immersed in a magnificent gorilla outfit!

Even Ian, however, could not have perpetrated the newspaper 'prank' that preceded the Melbourne third Test on 29 December. Local readers saw huge headlines proclaiming a first-person piece by Botham which began: 'There's nothing second-class about this England cricket team, including me. Which is why we are well on the way to achieving the 6–0 series win that we've been planning.

'After we deal with you, perhaps you may all get fair dinkum, discard your eskies and hats and head down to the nets for a bit of practice.

'For after we finish your lot this weekend, you'll need a completely new side.'

The first paragraph was the sort of sentiment to which Ian would undoubtedly subscribe, but when the quotes lapsed into 'fair dinkum' and 'eskies' (ice boxes, incidentally), it became abundantly clear that the story was a clumsy fabrication, an imaginary interview. If only the unnamed author had stuck to straightforward English, he might have got away with it!

The Melbourne Test, in the event, brought more shocks, but this time for England. First Australia built a score of 243 for four with Graeme Wood (the best batsman for misjudging a run since Compton and Boycott) hitting 100, then tumbled next day to 258, Botham being back among the wickets with three for 68. Then England again struggled from the quicksand of 3 for two. Only twenties from Gooch, Gower and Botham brought them to 143.

Even with Australia out for 167 second time around, Botham again being the main destroyer with three for 41, England's victory target of 283 was made impossible as they again started suicidally at 6 for two.

They were all out for 179, and lost by 103 runs – the first defeat in Brearley's sixteen Tests as skipper. An aggregate 135,000 had seen the match and the Ashes were at last ablaze. Hogg was the Australian hero. He had taken five wickets in each of England's last four innings and, so far, 27 in the series. He was the antithesis of Ian Botham, an asthmatic condition generally

The dismal Perth Test when 11 and 30 were poor compensation for bowling figures of nought for 100.

142

limiting him to four-over bursts, his best ball skidding into the batsman from outside off-stump.

Yet it was his fast bowling partner, Alan Hurst, who destroyed England's first innings in what had become a crucial fourth Test in Adelaide. England were all out for 152 and Australia 56 for one by stumps on the first day. It would have been even worse but for yet another typically bold and brave piece of batting by Botham. He came in at 51 for four and was ninth out at 141 for a magnificent 59.

Then, when Australia had advanced to 178 for two on the second day, again he lifted England with an athletic short leg catch to remove Rick Darling, a ball for Toohey which induced an edged catch and a brilliant slip catch off the captain Yallop when the ball appeared to have passed him.

Australia's eventual lead was limited to 142 when it might have been so much more. Although on top, they could have been in a perfect position to turn the series upside down by levelling

More Perth misfortune. Ian makes a full-blooded drive off Yardley, but the ball skies for a catch in the second innings.

at two-all. England still had a huge shock when Hogg removed Boycott with the first ball of their second innings, but they then dug in for the next eleven and a half hours to total 346 spread over 146 overs, with Randall reviving memories of his 174 in the Melbourne Centenary Test by hitting 150.

Australia were left on the last day four and a half hours to get 205. In cold print it might have appeared easy, but Emburey and Miller enjoyed so much turn with their spin that the Aussies capitulated for III. England were 3–1 ahead in the series, the Ashes assured.

The jubilant Brearley declared: 'This was the best fightback in a Test that I've ever played in. We realised after losing the third Test and getting off to a bad start here that the whole tour could fall apart.'

But Brearley was bitterly criticised in the Australian Press for condoning the go-slow batting of England's marathon second innings which, for most of the time, was an exercise in saving the match. It may have seemed harsh back home in England – he had, after all, secured the Ashes – but against the increasing enthusiasm for Packer cricket with its paraphernalia of floodlights, multi-coloured clothing and inspired television coverage, the Ashes series was beginning to assume the identity of a supporting B-movie.

The first day of the fifth Test in Adelaide, however, was probably the most exciting of the series. Everything happened. England slumped to 27 for five and were rescued yet again by Botham. He was ninth out at 147, having hit 74 of the 129 added while he was at the wicket. When Australia batted, Rick Darling was hit under the heart by Bob Willis's fifth ball and it produced the worst pandemonium since Peter Lever felled Ewan Chatfield in New Zealand four years earlier. Every available auxiliary force ran on to the field, John Emburey applied mouth-to-mouth resuscitation and Darling, his tongue at one stage wrapped down his throat, not unnaturally survived. Botham, unimpressed, paced back and then took a wicket in his first and second overs and Australia were left at close of play exactly 100 behind England's 169.

Mercifully, Darling recovered so quickly that he was able to bat next day but, with Botham as usual leading the way with four for 42, Australia could only amass 164. Even then their hopes of yet coming back to square the series remained alive as they reduced England to 132 for six in their second innings.

The improbable alliance of Bob Taylor and Geoff Miller put paid to such ambitions as they added 135 for the seventh wicket, Taylor tragically glancing the ball to be caught behind three runs short of the first century of a career begun in 1960. Miller's 64 made not a few of us feel somewhat guilty about uncomplimentary opinions of his England status, not least myself earlier in this book, although I remain unconvinced that he is of proven Test class.

Australia's chosen players certainly did not look of proven Test standard as their second innings crumbled from 115 for two to 160 all out. England, by a massive 205 runs, had won the match and clinched a series that was now stone-dead. That Yallop's men were then to win the three one-day internationals 2–1, beating England at their own game, was completely

Conquering hero. Ian salutes a catch by Gower off his bowling in the Melbourne Test, but the match was to be England's one disaster.

inconsequential and evidence only that Brearley's players were tired and anxious to go home with a job well done.

So much became obvious as Brearley clashed with Botham and John Lever during one of the internationals, with skipper and players swearing at each other over lack of commitment.

Brearley, who would stand out as one of England's greatest captains if his batting ability remotely matched his qualities of leadership, exhorted his side to one last effort and the sixth Test was duly taken at Sydney by nine wickets as the Australians reached rock-bottom. Never had England beaten Australia by so devastating a margin as 5–1 . . . and yet the series left many awkward, unanswerable questions.

With nearly 20 top Australians signed up with Kerry Packer, England had achieved their successes against a theoretical Australian third XI, so just how shallow was their 5–1 win? Australian pitches had not played true and England's batting had been heavily suspect with only two centuries – by Randall and Gower – in a six-Test series. How would they fare against a full-strength West Indies or Pakistan in the World Cup?

Such imponderables were not part of Ian Botham's thinking as he flew home on 17 February to see, for the first time, his second child, Sarah, born fourteen days earlier in Doncaster. He had the comfortable satisfaction of knowing he had conquered Australia. He had the third best batting average (29·10) although he went in sixth; he had been joint top wicket-taker (23) with Geoff Miller; and, with Graham Gooch, had taken the most catches (nine).

The summer of 1979 would almost certainly establish him as the most successful bowler in the history of Test cricket. For, after Australia, he had taken his haul of Test wickets to 87 in seventeen Tests and only injury, illness or incredible loss of form would prevent him beating the fastest ton of Test wickets – by West Indian Andy Roberts in 21 matches. With India the opposition, the Roberts record seemed sure to fall.

Ian, in fact, was about to take revenge on the very bowler who had whacked him in the face some five years earlier at Taunton on 12 June 1974 and aroused a furious young lion on the trail to cricketing immortality.

One of the few not to fail as England's first innings in Melbourne folded for a dismal 143. He was third top scorer with only 22.

Overleaf: Glory at Edgbaston: 3 June 1978 with 100 against Pakistan.

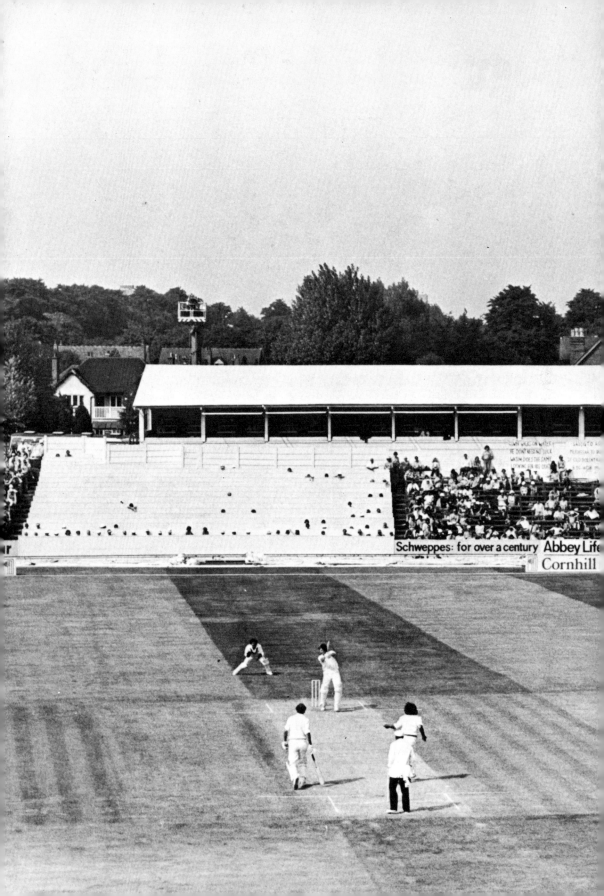

Figuratively Speaking

1973

John Player League

John Player League	Batting	Bowling	
Sussex (Hove)	2	3–0–22–0	
Surrey (Oval)	2	4–0–14–1	

1974

Championship and other first-class games

Lancs (Taunton)	13	–	3–0–15–0	
Sussex (Hove)	26	–	9–3–29–0	6–1–9–0
Gloucs (Bristol)	2	1	14–1–51–1	18–4–40–0
Yorks (Bath)	8	–	14–5–30–1	4–0–10–0
Northants (Northampton)	1	no 0	14–2–39–1	
Essex (Taunton)	21	9	9–1–26–0	
Middx (Taunton)	59	11		
Essex (Westcliff)	6	4	2–0–9–0	
Glam (Swansea)	25	–	5–1–5–0	11·4–4–22–2
Notts (Trent Bridge)	0	14	19·5–4–61–3	
Worcs (Worcester)	12	no 6	11–5–19–3	6–5–4–1
Leics (Weston)	39	4	28·2–8–59–5	23–6–58–2
Warwicks (Weston)	38	1	16–4–35–1	10–4–21–1
Gloucs (Weston)	41	no 9	15–1–39–3	6·4–0–23–1
Hants (Bournemouth)	20	–	13–3–48–0	
Derbys (Derby)	30	–	20–8–28–2	
Oxford Univ (Oxford)	–	2	3·2–1–10–0	
Pakistanis (Bath)	7	32	21–2–76–2	6·1–3–13–1

Runs 441, average 16·96 **Wickets** 30 for 779, average 25·96

John Player League

Sussex (Taunton)	18	8–1–16–2	
Gloucs (Bristol)	–	8–0–42–1	
Yorks (Bath)	–	6·3–0–43–1	
Derbys (Derby)	29	8–1–41–2	
Worcs (Worcester)	30	8–1–28–1	
Middx (Taunton)	no 4	8–0–43–0	
Notts (Trent Bridge)	no 10	8–1–19–0	
Glam (Swansea)	10	2–0–5–0	
Lancs (Torquay)	6		

Essex (Taunton)	0		8–0–44–0
Leics (Leicester)	15		

Runs 122, average 17·42   **Wickets** 7 for 281, average 40·14

Benson and Hedges Cup

Hants (Taunton)	3		11–0–52–1
Hants (Taunton)	no 45		11–3–33–2 (gold award)
Leics (Leicester)	18		9–1–60–0

Gillette Cup

Essex (Westcliff)	no 15		12–2–26–0
Surrey (Taunton)	–		12–0–53–0
Kent (Canterbury)	19		9–0–24–2

1975

Championship and other first-class games

Sussex (Taunton)	0	–	15–5–30–3	9–0–32–0
Northants (Northampton)	0	2	11–3–19–0	6·2–3–16–0
Middx (Lord's)	2	–	27–4–66–1	
Gloucs (Bristol)	–	no 4	21–7–37–3	17–5–53–2
Oxford Univ (Oxford)	44	no 33	20–4–53–3	22–6–54–1
Derbys (Bath)	65	no 26	11·3–3–17–2	23–4–55–1
Surrey (Bath)	21	16	19–5–46–3	13–3–29–1
Leics (Leicester)	0	27	21–2–68–2	27–7–76–2
Warwick (Edgbaston)	–	16	14–2–45–2	15·1–4–29–2
Yorks (Harrogate)	5	0	13–1–55–0	15–6–46–1
Lancs (Old Trafford)	0	8	27–8–69–5	
Northants (Taunton)	45	12	14–3–41–2	11–1–57–2
Worcs (Weston)	1	1	23·2–6–59–4	10–2–53–2
Hants (Weston)	14	9	17–3–46–3	9–0–33–1
Australians (Taunton)	8	0	21–4–66–0	1·1–0–4–0
Essex (Leyton)	no 23	11	9–2–33–1	9–1–30–0
Gloucs (Taunton)	11	–	21–5–55–2	4–0–14–0
Notts (Taunton)	–	–	9–1–55–0	
Kent (Folkestone)	6	54	14–1–51–0	7–1–34–1
Glam (Cardiff)	23	25	16–7–27–1	22–6–51–3
Essex (Taunton)	17	10	11–1–30–1	8–2–15–2
Glam (Taunton)	–	45	8–2–15–0	14–1–40–3

Runs 584, average 18·25   **Wickets** 62 for 1,704, average 27·48

John Player League

Essex (Chelmsford)	3	8–0–32–2
Gloucs (Bristol)	–	8–1–46–0
Leics (Yeovil)	24	8–2–23–0
Surrey (Guildford)	6	6–1–14–1
Derbys (Bath)	no 38	8–0–33–2
Notts (Bath)	26	8–2–27–1
Yorks (Bradford)	12	8–0–29–1
Lancs (Old Trafford)	21	6·2–1–40–1
Northants (Torquay)	0	8–2–19–1
Sussex (Hove)	4	5–0–12–2
Hants (Weston)	12	8–0–61–3
Warwicks (Edgbaston)	no 15	8–0–44–2
Middx (Lord's)	–	4–0–21–0
Glam (Taunton)	no 16	8–0–38–0
Kent (Canterbury)	7	8–1–34–3
Worcs (Taunton)	4	8–2–37–2

Runs 188, average 17·09   **Wickets** 21 for 510, average 24·28

Benson and Hedges Cup

Glam (Taunton)	–	7–3–11–0
Surrey (Oval)	11	11–0–51–1
Gloucs (Street)	–	11–4–25–2
Hants (Bournemouth)	4	11–5–29–2
Hants (Southampton)	7	11–2–56–3

Gillette Cup

Surrey (Oval)	21	12–2–46–2
Derbys (Taunton)	1	12–2–39–1

1976

Prudential Trophy

West Indies (Scarborough)	1	3–0–26–1
West Indies (Edgbaston)	20	3–0–31–1

Championship and other first-class games

Camb Univ (Fenners)	no 16	no 6	18·3–2–75–4	6–0–22–0
Hants (Taunton)	9	–	28–4–79–1	23–5–76–2
Glam (Cardiff)	1	–	16–4–43–4	37–7–103–4
Sussex (Hove)	6	97	29·5–5–113–2	
Surrey (Guildford)	9	2	16–3–52–2	7–1–22–2
West Indians (Taunton)	56	0	18–5–72–2	18–3–66–0
Gloucs (Taunton)	13	3	16·1–6–25–6	37·1–6–125–5
Worcs (Worcester)	11	1	20–0–77–4	20–2–82–2
Middx (Bath)	9	–	17–2–56–0	
Northants (Northampton)	34	17	26–2–109–1	
Warwicks (Taunton)	36	no 36	28–7–80–1	11–0–50–1
Derbys (Chesterfield)	33	4	22–3–69–0	7–1–34–1
Yorks (Taunton)	52	31	21–5–74–5	3–0–12–0
Hants (Bournemouth)	44	0	12–5–16–6	2–0–10–0
Notts (Trent Bridge)	80	no 167	14–2–59–1	13–4–16–1
Lancs (Weston)	25	6	7–1–22–2	2–0–6–0
Glam (Weston)	23	–	14–4–49–3	6–2–15–0
Kent (Taunton)	rtd hurt 12	–	8–3–26–0	
Essex (Leyton)	58	37	20–4–60–3	6–0–42–0
Leics (Taunton)	88	0	14–2–43–1	

Runs 1,022, average 34·06   **Wickets** 66 for 1,880, average 28·48

John Player League

Worcs (Worcester)	39	7–0–27–1
Sussex (Taunton)	11	8–1–22–1
Essex (Yeovil)	32	8–0–43–2
Leics (Leicester)	5	8–2–29–1
Hants (Portsmouth)	8	7–0–29–0
Middx (Bath)	43	8–0–41–4
Northants (Northampton)	28	8–0–53–3
Warwicks (Taunton)	–	8–2–23–2
Derbys (Heanor)	no 15	8–1–37–2
Yorks (Glastonbury)	18	8–0–33–0
Notts (Trent Bridge)	37	8–1–44–1
Lancs (Weston)	8	7–0–27–0
Surrey (Taunton)	16	8–0–32–3
Kent (Taunton)	46	8–1–28–2
Glamorgan (Cardiff)	9	7–0–41–2

Runs 315, average 24·23   **Wickets** 24 for 509, average 21·20

Benson and Hedges Cup

Worcs (Taunton)	3	11–1–45–2	
Gloucs (Bristol)	0	11–2–31–1	
Leics (Taunton)	no 43	8·4–2–21–1	
Minor Counties (Cheltenham)	10	11–2–24–2	

Gillette Cup

Warwicks (Edgbaston)	3	6–1–24–1	

1977

England v Australia

3rd Test (Trent Bridge)	25	–	20–5–74–5	25–5–60–0
4th Test (Headingley)	–	0	11–3–21–5	17–3–47–0

MCC

Middx (Lord's)	no 53	–	18–5–40–3	8–0–19–2
Australians (Lord's)	no 10	0	16–5–31–1	15–5–43–2

Championship and other first-class games

Glam (Taunton)	27	–	28·2–9–71–5	
Notts (Bath)	69	1	16·5–2–40–2	13–2–42–1
Australians (Bath)	59	no 39	15–2–48–1	22–6–98–4
Hants (Southampton)	0	9	34–7–95–2	3–0–4–0
Glam (Cardiff)	5	–	14–4–49–1	22–5–75–3
Yorks (Harrogate)	11	14	34·3–8–112–4	11–2–46–2
Leics (Leicester)	0	–	29–8–77–4	29–7–84–2
Sussex (Hove)	62	–	42–5–111–4	23·5–10–50–6
Hants (Taunton)	114	40	21–2–69–4	16–5–43–4
Sussex (Taunton)	39	14	25·2–12–58–6	23–5–78–2
Warwicks (Edgbaston)	0	59	30–6–76–5	21–2–74–1
Worcs (Taunton)	7	10	22–4–62–2	16–3–42–2
Northants (Weston)	44	27	28–2–116–1	6–0–28–2

First-class runs 738, average 30·75   **Wickets** 88 for 1,938, average 22·53

John Player League

Leics (Taunton)	17	8–0–32–1	
Essex (Chelmsford)	1	4–0–22–0	
Notts (Bath)	20	8–0–45–0	
Middx (Lord's)	44	8–0–42–2	
Yorks (Scarborough)	10	7–0–13–1	
Lancs (Old Trafford)	55	8–0–33–2	
Hants (Street)	69	8–0–38–2	
Surrey (Byfleet)	9	8–0–30–2	
Worcs (Bristol)	–	8–3–16–2	
Sussex (Hove)	14	8–0–23–0	
Northants (Weston)	15	7–0–27–0	

Benson and Hedges Cup

Gloucs (Bristol)	9	10–1–33–0
Leics (Taunton)	20	11–2–36–2
Hants (Bournemouth)	21	10·2–3–20–2
Lancs (Bath)	3	10·4–2–46–0

Gillette Cup

Northumberland (Taunton)	no 91	12–3–37–2 (man of match)
Derbys (Ilkeston)	25	9–1–23–2

England Tour 1977/78

Pakistan

United Bank (Faisalabad)	–	0	12–5–26–1	4–0–20–0
Governor's XI (Peshawar)	–	no 22	4–1–11–0	4–0–12–0
Punjab (Bahawalpur)	–	–	8–0–52–1	9–2–31–2

One-day games

Pakistan (Sahiwal)	no 15	7–0–39–3
Harib Bank (Lahore)	15	5–1–7–2
Pakistan (Sialkot)	no 17	6·7–0–21–1
Pakistan (Lahore)	11	7–0–41–0
Sind XI (Karachi)	47	3–0–14–0

New Zealand

1st Test (Wellington)	7	19	12·6–2–27–2	9·3–3–13–2
2nd Test (Christchurch)	103	no 30	24·7–6–73–5	7–1–38–3
3rd Test (Auckland)	53	–	34–4–109–5	13–1–51–0
Auckland (Auckland)	33	–	6–0–36–0	8–2–27–1
Canterbury (Christchurch)	0	no 126	11–3–28–3	7–1–45–0
Otago (Dunedin)	0	no 4	17–4–33–3	19·4–6–58–7

One-day games

N. Districts (Hamilton)	23	5–1–16–1

1978

England v Pakistan

1st Test (Edgbaston)	100	–	15–4–52–1	17–3–47–0
2nd Test (Lord's)	108	–	5–2–17–0	20·5–8–34–8
3rd Test (Headingley)	4	–	18–2–59–4	

Prudential Trophy

Pakistan (Old Trafford)	31	8–1–17–2
Pakistan (Oval)	1	11–2–36–1

England v New Zealand

1st Test (Oval)	22	–	22–7–58–1	19–2–46–3
2nd Test (Trent Bridge)	8	–	21–9–34–6	24–7–59–3
3rd Test (Lord's)	21	–	38–12–103–6	18·1–4–39–5

Prudential Trophy

New Zealand (Scarborough)	3	11–1–43–1
New Zealand (Old Trafford)	34	7–0–24–1

MCC

Middx (Lord's)	–	–	17·3–5–43–5 (including hat-trick)	

Championship and other first-class games

Derbys (Burton)	0	–	23·1–8–48–3	
Glam (Taunton)	12	–	20–4–70–1	18·2–3–66–6
Gloucs (Taunton)	86	–	22–3–53–5	26–4–101–2
Lancs (Bath)	14	0	15–5–29–3	35–9–86–3
Yorks (Taunton)	27	5	23–2–92–2	22–4–52–2
Glam (Cardiff)	3	–	20–5–61–7	11–3–26–1
Essex (Colchester)	44	4	19–4–30–2	13–1–47–2
Warwicks (Weston)	20	–	21·5–7–43–6	17·3–5–37–3
Middx (Taunton)	9	11	19–1–79–2	7–0–36–2
Worcs (Worcester)	–	40	33·4–9–86–6	3·2–0–9–0

First-class runs 538, average 26·90   **Wickets** 100 for 1,640, average 16·40

John Player League

Kent (Maidstone)	–	6–1–13–2
Worcs (Taunton)	3	6–0–26–2
Surrey (Yeovil)	–	7·5–2–16–1
Lancs (Bath)	52	8–1–30–3
Yorks (Bristol)	30	8–1–39–0
Glam (Cardiff)	no 7	5–0–20–1
Warwicks (Weston)	–	8–1–26–2
Middx (Taunton)	17	8–0–30–1
Essex (Taunton)	45	8–0–38–2

Runs 154, average 30·80   **Wickets** 14 for 238, average 17·00

Benson and Hedges Cup

Glam (Cardiff)	2	11–2–35–1
Worcs (Taunton)	22	11–3–29–3
Universities (Taunton)	–	11–2–16–4 (gold award)
Sussex (Hove)	54	11–1–29–1 (gold award)
Kent (Taunton)	15	11–1–39–3

Gillette Cup

Warwicks (Taunton)	11	12–2–37–1
Glam (Cardiff)	no 15	12–1–44–2
Kent (Canterbury)	24	8·5–0–33–1
Essex (Taunton)	7	12–1–48–2
Sussex (Lord's)	80	12–1–65–2

England Tour 1978/79

Australia

1st Test (Brisbane)	49	–	12·1–40–3	26–5–95–3
2nd Test (Perth)	11	30	11–2–46–0	11–1–54–0
3rd Test (Melbourne)	22	10	20·1–4–68–3	15–4–41–3
4th Test (Sydney)	59	6	28–3–87–2	
5th Test (Adelaide)	74	7	11·4–0–42–4	14–4–37–1
6th Test (Sydney)	23	–	9·7–1–57–4	

State matches

New South Wales (Sydney)	56	–	9–2–41–0	17·2–6–51–5
Queensland (Brisbane)	6	–	12–1–66–3	20–3–70–5
Western Australia (Perth)	4	4	9–3–16–4	13·5–4–37–4

One-day internationals

Melbourne	–	4·5–2–16–3
Melbourne	31	7·6–0–58–0
Melbourne	13	5·5–0–30–1

One-day games

Q'nsland Country (Bundaberg)	22	7–0–34–0
Tasmania (Launceston)	61	6–0–18–1

Acknowledgments

Bristol Evening Post 26, 37, 52, 55, 108–109, 110 left, 112, 113, 121, 126–127, 131, 133; Central Press, London 44, 70, 92; Christchurch Press Co., New Zealand 72, 76; E-Pix, Taunton 107, 108, 110 right, 123; Hamlyn Group – Tony Duffy 4–5, 106; Hamlyn Group – John Webb 21 top, 27, 79, 93; Alan Lockyer, Taunton 20; New Zealand Herald, Auckland 78; Press Association, London 45, 60, 61, 63, 89, 97, 98–99, 104, 129, 136, 139; Rank Radio International, Plymouth 21 bottom; Sport and General Press Agency, London 28 top right, 30, 116, 119; Sporting Pictures (UK), London 80, 87 bottom, 94.

The remaining photographs were supplied by Patrick Eagar.

Index